How Can I Have a Harelip if I Am not a Rabbit?

Amy Laschinske

Copyright © 2024 Amy Laschinske

All rights reserved. No part of this book may be reproduced or transmitted in any form or by any means, electronic or mechanical, including photocopying, recording or by any information storage and retrieval system without permission in writing from the publisher.

Writing Rabbit—Massillon, Ohio
ISBN: 979-8-3305-6863-5
Title: *How Can I Have a Harelip if I Am not a Rabbit*
Author: Amy Laschinske
Digital distribution | 2024
Paperback | 2024

Published in the United States by New Book Authors Publishing

Acknowledgements

To all my friends and family, I want to express my deepest gratitude for your support and encouragement on my book writing journey. I wish I had the room to thank each of you personally. I hope I make it clear how much I love all of you.

Chapter One
The Slide Trombone

I can still recall the exact moment of my life when I realized I was different from the other children. It occurred when I was in fourth grade at Lake Cable Elementary School when I found that I could not play the slide trombone. I know what you're thinking, millions of people cannot play the slide trombone and still go on to lead long and fulfilling lives. But I assure you, to a fourth grader who wanted nothing more from life at the time, it was indeed a big deal.

My family had just moved into the school district, so I was the NEW girl. Anyone who has ever experienced being the new girl knows that it is one of the most miserable things to go through in your life. First, you walk into a classroom full of complete strangers who immediately stop what they are doing to stare at you. There is utter silence as you make your way to the teacher's desk and hand in your transfer papers. Then, just in case there was anyone not paying attention to you, the teacher announces to the class, "Boys and girls, we have a new student with us this year."

Now, even the class moron who was ignoring you while trying to stick his nose in the pencil sharpener, becomes aware of your presence.

"Please take the empty desk next to Cindy."

As you make your way down the aisle, Cindy is hoping you fall and hit your head causing you to fall into a coma thus leaving the desk next to her vacant. You take your seat and wait for the novelty of being the new girl wears off. This is where I was at in my life when the slide trombone issue arose.

We were a few weeks into the school year when we started studying band instruments. The teacher, Mrs. Zink, said we would be listening to all kinds of instruments and at the end of the week anyone who wanted could try out for the school band. I wasn't too terribly interested in any of this until I noticed that most of the class got excited about joining the band. A lightbulb went off in my head. This could be my chance to fit in. Surely bandmates stuck together, didn't they?

Each day, Mrs. Zink would put a picture of a different band instrument up on the board and then we would listen to a recording of that instrument. I heard flutes and saxophones and every other instrument you could think of. By Thursday, I was starting to panic because I hadn't decided on what instrument I wanted to play. Listening to my classmates, it seemed that most girls favored the flute while the boys liked the drums or the tuba. I wasn't wild about either one. Leave it to me to want desperately to fit in yet still be different.

Then on Friday, I heard it, the instrument that was going to save me from a life of despair. The slide trombone. No one else seemed interested in the trombone making it the perfect choice for me. I would join the band with my classmates yet still maintain my individuality.

I went home Friday afternoon and drove my poor

parents nuts with my constant chatter about the slide trombone. I could work it into any conversation my parents tried to have with me that weekend.

"So, Amy, did you clean your room like I asked?"

"Yes Mom. I need to make room for my new trombone."

Or my dad asking me if I wanted to ride along to the store with him.

"Sure Dad, although I won't have time for this sort of thing once I start my trombone lessons."

My parents could have convinced a judge that it was justifiable child abuse if they would have duct taped my mouth shut and locked me in a closet for the entire weekend. I had convinced myself that I was going to become a world-famous slide trombone player and live a fabulous life of wealth and fame. Or, at the very least, be part of the "in" crowd among fourth graders at Lake Cable Elementary School.

I was on pins and needles on Monday waiting for the meeting after school to get signed up for the band. When three o'clock finally rolled around, I sprinted to the gym where I found my parents waiting for me. First, we had to sit through some guy rattling on about various ways my parents could finance this childhood endeavor.

Finally, he said to go to the table where the instrument of our choice was waiting. I ran to the slide trombone table and was shocked to see that I was not the first in line. Right in front of me stood the class moron I mentioned earlier. He never figured out how to stick his nose in the pencil sharpener, but he did manage to get his finger stuck in the sink in the bathroom. I just know he grew up to be one of those guys that got his penis stuck in some household appliance. I waited impatiently why he tooted on the horn a few times and the instructor talked with his parents. They got him signed up for lessons and finally it was my turn.

The instructor took one look at me and whispered something to my parents who asked me if I would rather go try out the drums, DRUMS? Were these folks out of their minds? Weren't they listening to all my grand ideas about becoming the best slide trombone player in the world? No way, it was going to be the slide trombone or nothing. Looking back on it now, I don't know why I was so obsessed with this instrument. It's not like I had ever played one before or even heard someone else play it. I mean quick, name the top five trombone players in the world. And, if the whole point of joining the band was to fit in, why not the drums? For some reason I had made up my mind it had to be the trombone.

The instructor shrugged his shoulders and handed me the horn. I brought the beautiful horn up to my lips and blew for all I was worth. Nothing. I tried again, and again nothing. I don't know how many times I blew into the damn thing trying to coax something remotely musical out of it but all I managed to do was spit all over it and make a noise like someone blowing their nose. My eyes filled with tears as I turned to my father and asked him why I couldn't make music. He gently explained that because of my cleft lip, I couldn't form a seal around the mouthpiece.

My parents tried to console me the best they could when we got home but I was heartbroken. I went to bed devastated. As I was lying there for a while, another problem started to nag at me. What was I going to tell all my classmates about why I wouldn't be joining the band? I had been bragging about it all week.

I ran several plans through my head. Maybe I could become a fourth-grade dropout. Nah, I'm pretty sure my parents weren't going to go for this plan. I got it, I'll fake my own death. I'll have my folks print an obituary in the newspaper, have a fake funeral, then move out of the state. Again, pretty sure this was going to be a tough sell. Finally, I came up with the best plan of all. It was beautiful in its simplicity and my parents wouldn't even have to know about it. I went to school on Tuesday and announced that I had decided that band was for sissies.

Chapter Two
Snorkel Nose

If I learned from the slide trombone that there were going to be physical limitations to having a harelip and cleft palate, I learned from the other kids that there was going to be social limitations as well.

I'm sure that everyone has a horror story about being made fun of from time to time during their childhood. But to a child with a disfiguring defect to their face, childhood becomes an endless nightmare. You've heard that children can be cruel, they can be downright evil at times. They can inflict an incredible amount of pain that some kids never recover from. Scars so deep that they can do serious, lasting damage.

Did you have a nickname while you were growing up? I hope it was a term of endearment bestowed upon you by your friends or family. My decidedly un-endearing nickname while I was growing up was Snorkel Nose. I am at a loss to explain why they chose Snorkel Nose. My nose, as a matter of fact, was flat. For that matter, my entire face was pretty flat. You would have thought they could have incorporated that flatness into a much more imaginative nickname. Even Flatface would have made more sense. My only excuse for them is that they were young.

The first time I heard it was during recess on my first day of junior high school. I was hanging out with a tall, skinny girl named Sue. She was my locker mate, and we had spent the morning trying to figure out how to work the combination on the locker. We laughed a lot, and she seemed to be a nice person, so I figured I was safe sticking with her. I hadn't yet experienced betrayal, but I was about to get a very painful lesson on the subject.

Sue and I were walking along the school yard when I noticed we had drawn a small crowd. I turned to face the seven or eight girls to see what they wanted.

Just then, Sue, my new best friend, walked toward the group and said, "This is the girl with the weird face I was telling you about."

They all started laughing and one of them called me Snorkel Nose.

I suppose it must have had a nice ring to it because it caught on like wildfire. Soon they were all chanting "Snorkel Nose, Snorkel Nose" at me. The tears that had begun falling down my cheeks only added to the fun for them. I turned away from my tormentors and started to run. Then, as if I wasn't humiliated enough, someone tripped me, and I fell flat on my face in the dirt much to the delight of my sadistic audience. I then became known as the Snorkel Nose Retard.

In a perfect world, I would be able to tell you that at least one of these girls stepped forward to see if I was alright. One out of eight who experienced a pang of remorse and came to my aid. Well, the world is an imperfect place and none of them did. I guess you never know true loneliness until you're the one being picked on.

Before they could heap any more abuse on me, the bell rang, and everyone headed inside. I picked myself up, wiped the blood off my chin, and headed to my next class in a daze. I was going to have to find a way to deal with these bullies or I would wind up bloodied and humiliated every day for the rest of my life. There had to be a way to get through these episodes that hurt less and did less damage to my very fragile self-esteem. But how? My swan dive into the dirt failed to impress anyone, so gaining their sympathy was out of the question. And what about Sue? How could she spend the whole morning being nice to me only to turn on me like she did? I was angry, hurt, and very confused. She was my locker mate for crying out loud!

I was at the age where I was just starting to understand how peer pressure worked. My only formal discussion on the subject was my mother asking me the age-old question about jumping off the bridge if everyone else did. If my first day of junior high was any indication about how the rest of my life was going to go, I would have happily jumped off the highest bridge I could find. I could employ Sue's method of coping and find someone more vulnerable than me to pick on. Let's see, I had big, thick glasses, braces on my teeth, and a cleft lip and palate. I was going to have to search far and wide to find someone more pathetic than me. What should I do next?

It couldn't have been too hard to tell that my first day of school had not gone well. My mom took one look at my torn, dirty clothes, and red puffy eyes and asked me if I wanted to talk about it. I have always tried to shield my mother from the worst of the hell I was going through because I knew how much it hurt her. So, I said "no," went to my room and cried myself to sleep. When my dad got home, he came into my room and asked me what happened. I poured out the whole pathetic story to him between my sobs. I told him I didn't know what to do to make the kids stop picking on me. He tried to sell me on the idea that I should ignore my tormentors and walk away. I pointed out that I had tried this approach and wound up going from Snorkel Nose to Snorkel Nose Retard in zero point five seconds.

My dad then imparted some wisdom to me that would change my life. He told me I had to learn to fight. Go after the one who was teasing me and beat the living daylights out of them. I hadn't considered this an option before because I was afraid I would get into trouble for fighting at school. Besides, I didn't really know how to fight. My dad must have figured out that things were only going to get worse for me if I didn't learn how to defend myself. I think he secretly hoped I would beat the hell out of anyone who ever hurt me.

So, my dad taught me how to box. I'm sure you will not find a chapter in any child rearing book about the techniques to teach your youngster how to throw a perfect punch, but my dad taught me to keep my hands up, back someone off with the jab and finally, how to deliver the knockout punch.

After dinner, he and I went to the basement to practice. Me jabbing him in the chest and ducking and weaving his pretend counter punches. My father did some boxing in his younger days, and I learned so much from him that night. I was beginning to see my dad in a whole new light. By the end of the evening, I was feeling a whole lot better. My dad was my new hero.

He only asked that I follow two rules. One, I was not to go looking to start trouble. Two, I had to try to walk away before I started swinging. He explained that fighting was not the answer and was only to be used as a last resort.

"What if I get in trouble at school for fighting?" I asked him.

"Tell your teacher to call me and I'll come to the school and straighten it out," he replied.

That night, as I lay in bed, I thought of how different things would have gone if I had gotten up and belted the girl who tripped me. I'll bet they would have thought twice about teasing me again. At the very least, they wouldn't have added the Retard to my name. I replayed the scene over and over in my head in slow motion. Me ramming my fist in the mouth of the girl who called me Snorkel Nose. Let someone else hurt instead of me for a change. The whole idea was enough to make me smile.

As I drifted off to sleep, I made a promise to myself that I would do as my father asked me. I was also sure that the next round of teasing would have a very different outcome.

Chapter Three
Kicking Ass

I can't recall Brenda's last name from junior high school, but I can recall that I laid quite an ass-whipping on her. As you might have guessed, she was the first one who bullied me after I instituted Operation Violence.

It started in the gym during activity period. When it was raining outside and you couldn't have recess, they crammed us all in the gym and called it activity period. I was sitting in the bleachers by myself watching all the other girls break off into their little groups to chat. I didn't mingle because I was already painfully shy. It didn't help that their Welcome Wagon committee that greeted me on my first day left something to be desired.

As I was sitting there, I noticed that Brenda and her friends were pointing at me and laughing. I've developed a sixth sense about spotting people who are talking about me. It starts with a sick feeling in your stomach that works its way up to your eyes and points you in the direction of those people. I call it a sixth sense; others would call it paranoia. I tried not to pay any attention when I saw Brenda and her gang making their way towards the bleachers where I sat.

When they sat down right beside me, I wanted so badly to believe that they were just trying to be friendly. I wished with all my heart that they would just introduce themselves and make small talk until the bell rang. What they had to say was anything but friendly.

After much goading and prodding, Brenda finally turned to me and said, "You're the Snorkel Nose Retard, aren't you?"

I glanced at her then quickly turned away as I felt the bitter tears of disappointment well up in my eyes. I gathered up my books to leave when Brenda pulled them from my arms and sent them scattering all over the gym floor. Needless to say, we were starting to draw a crowd. Try as I might, I could not stop the tears from spilling over and running down my cheeks. Brenda's critical mistake was to then call me Snorkel Nose Retard Crybaby.

I don't know if it was the addition of this last adjective to an already loathed nickname, or the fact that I had decided that I had fulfilled my father's request to try and walk away, but something deep inside me snapped. I turned to Brenda and belted her squarely in the mouth. Not satisfied with that, I jumped on top of her and proceeded to beat her into a bloody mess. I must give one of her friend's kudos, she tried to pull me off Brenda and got a black eye for her trouble.

It was Brenda's misfortune to be the first person I ever hit because I released all the fury that had been building in me for years. Completely enraged, I set out to punish her. I punished her for the girls who had made my first day so miserable. I punished her for the betrayal of locker mate Sue. Hell, I even punished her for the fact that I could not play the damn slide trombone.

I don't know what came over me, I could have gone on beating her for hours, but the bell rang signifying the end of activity period, so I stopped my activity. I stepped away from her breathing hard and wild-eyed. I must have been a scary sight because I turned to someone and growled, "Pick up my fucking books and hand them to me."

This is exactly what she did as she must have thought it would be a bad idea to argue with me at this point.

I looked around at the crowd and noticed no one was laughing at me this time. They were all staring at me with their mouths hanging open. I bent down to where Brenda was lying on the floor bloodied and crying and said loudly, "Never call me Snorkel Nose again." With one last glance at the crowd to let them know I meant that for all of them, I walked out of the gym.

I stopped at the restroom to wash Brenda's blood off my fist and splash some cold water on my face. What the hell had just happened back there? I was both completely thrilled and utterly horrified at what I had done. I stood there a second and decided I had done the right thing. I also allowed myself a small smile. I hoped I had put the name Snorkel Nose to rest for good!

Not knowing what else to do, I headed off to my English class. I could not ignore the fact that everyone was talking about the fight. Rumor had it that they had taken Brenda to the nurse's station. I wondered how long it would be before someone came for me. About halfway through class, an office aid knocked on the door and informed the teacher that I was wanted in the principal's office.

As I made my way to the office, I felt like I was marching to my own execution. I prayed my dad would hold up his end of our deal and come to my rescue. Filled with dread and terrified, I walked into the office.

The scene that awaited me there almost made me faint.

Not only was the principal, Mr. Duda, there, so was Brenda and her mother. Her mother glared at me as I walked by, and I was certain I was a goner. I wondered what horrible punishment was about to be inflicted on me. It didn't help that hanging on the wall behind the principal was a large, wooden, paddle that Mr. Duda used to keep order in our school. I looked over at Brenda and saw I had done quite a number on her. Both of her eyes were swollen, and her lip was getting fatter by the second. She was toying with an ice pack in her hands and would not look at me.

Mr. Duda said, "Amy, we would like to hear your side of the story."

I told them what happened and when I was done, Brenda's mother turned to her and said, "If you were making fun of this girl's face, you deserved the beating you got."

She then told Mr. Duda that she was sorry for wasting his time and that she had not been given the whole story when Brenda called home. Then she made Brenda apologize to ME. I must admit that it was sweet having the tide turn in my favor and watching Brenda squirm. Mr. Duda thanked me for coming in and told me I was free to go.

I left the office to the sound of Brenda's mother giving her holy hell. I stood in the hallway and listened for a minute then I walked away laughing. Poor Brenda was having herself a hell of a day. I wanted to weep with relief that I was off the hook but took pleasure in Brenda's misery. I was stunned by the turn of events. I couldn't wait to get home and tell my dad all about it.

Then, just when I thought things couldn't get any

better, an amazing thing happened. After class, a few of the kids gathered around me and asked me what happened in the office. I couldn't believe they actually wanted to talk to me. I had gotten used to being ignored for the most part. I told them about the office visit and when I finished, they were laughing with me. WITH me, not AT me.

I began to realize that I had taken an important step in handling my problem. It wasn't that I had kicked Brenda's ass, although that was very satisfying, I had defended myself. I had asked to be treated with a little basic, human respect. I was not going to allow myself to be anyone's verbal punching bag again. For the first time since I entered Sauder Junior High School, I walked out with a smile on my face.

When I told my dad about it that evening, he looked me sternly in the eye and said, "You tried to walk away first didn't you?"

I returned his gaze and said, "Yes Sir."

Then he laughed and high-fived me. Even my mom, who didn't approve of the fighting, couldn't help but laugh with us.

Chapter Four
Thank You, Janis Ian

I want to take a moment to pay tribute to a lady I consider a friend even though I have never met her…Janis Ian. Her song, *At Seventeen,* literally helped save my life when I was twelve years old. Please go and listen to it before reading any further so you will better understand what I'm talking about here. It's a beautiful yet haunting song about ugly, misfit girls, like me.

I had been going through a particularly rough stretch at school when the torment had reached an all-time high. The fighting and humiliation came often, and it was draining the life out of me. I may have been winning the physical battles, but I was losing the emotional wars. I felt ugly, alone, and the pain was becoming unbearable. One day, I decided that the only way for me to end the hellish agony I was in was to take my own life. I was certain that no one else could understand how I was feeling.

I sat down with pen and paper and wrote a suicide note trying to explain myself and apologizing to my parents for being born with a cleft lip and palate. I wanted them to know that my killing myself was not their fault. Next, I went to the medicine cabinet and grabbed a handful of pills from every prescription bottle I could find. I gathered them all and took them back to my room and laid them on my bed. I stared at them for a long time. Would it hurt? Would I get sick? I carefully considered the fact that there would be no turning back if I decided to do this. I stashed the note and the pills and decided to wait until I was home alone to put my plan in motion.

I was lying in bed one evening listening to the radio. From the first line, *"I learned the truth at seventeen, that love was meant for beauty queens,"* I felt like Janis was singing it directly to me. At twelve, I was sure I was the only girl who felt ugly, alone, and rejected, but here was this magical song telling me this was not the case. I listened to the radio every chance I got wanting to hear that song again and eventually I did. I begged my mom to buy me a copy of the record and one day she came home with it.

I went straight to my room and played it repeatedly for hours. I played it until I knew every word. I knew the words to other songs, but this was different, I felt the words of this one. Janis sang of pain, and I had felt that pain firsthand and it helped to know that there was someone else who understood.

Janis and I spent many a night in my room feeling sorry for ourselves. It got so that after a really hard day, I could listen to the song and feel better. It became a healing process for me. If no one else understood what I was going through, Janis did, and I could count on her every time.

I did find myself home alone one evening and two things stopped me from killing myself. One, my parents had already lost one child, my brother Mark had died from a medical condition when I was four and though I didn't fully understand at that age, I felt their sadness over it. Two, Janis Ian sent a song to me that reached out and touched the heart of a scared, lonely, girl who really needed it at the time. I flushed the pills, tore up the note and found the courage to continue living.

So, thank you Janis Ian, your song truly helped save my life. Your gift as a singer songwriter that you shared with the world, is one that I could never repay you for.

Chapter Five
Six Wins, One Loss

I ended up having a few more minor battles in junior high. As near as I can tell, my boxing record stands at about six and one. It's that one loss that I want to talk about here because it's the one I have never forgotten.

When you decide to bully someone, my advice is to avoid anyone who has any form of birth defect. There is a ball of rage inside of us that when tapped into, releases a fury the likes of which Satan himself has never seen. All of our lives we have been tormented because we are different, and one day someone hits the release valve, and all of that pent up rage comes pouring out of us. Someone usually winds up hurt and it will usually be you. But this time, I was the one who needed ice packs.

I was in a field goofing off with some friends. Two neighbor boys came riding by on their bikes when one of them yelled, "Hey Flatnose, come sniff my ass."

It wasn't hard to figure out who he was talking to. We took off after them and caught up with them a few blocks down the street. His name was Mark Richards, and his younger sister was a friend of mine. He was two years older than me and had never bothered me before. I figured he was just showing off for his buddy. Mark and I circled each other like two prize fighters.

"You're going to look pretty stupid getting your ass kicked by a girl," I taunted him.

"Bring it on, Flatnose," he replied.

I was trying to remember everything my father had taught me about boxing. I kept my hands up near my face and was looking for a clear punch. At the exact same moment, we both threw a punch, and our knuckles collided with the force of a train wreck. Forgetting everything my dad taught me; I dropped my right hand down to cradle my injured left hand. This gave Mark the break he was looking for and he slammed his fist into my right eye. I reeled two steps backward and swung wildly but missed. This gave Mark the opportunity to punch me square in my left eye. This time, I went down for the count. He had opened a pretty good gash above my left eye and blood went everywhere. It must have scared the hell out of him because he and his buddy hopped on their bikes and took off.

My friends helped me to my feet and half walked; half carried me home. When we reached my house, they told my mom what happened, and she went nuts. She had me to lie on the couch, got a towel and two ice bags for my eyes. Then she got out the phone book and called the Richard's house.

I had never seen my mother this angry before. She told Mark's mother that she didn't appreciate her son making fun of me. She ought to call the police on her son for assaulting me. What kind of people raised their son to hit a girl? If I needed stitches, she would make sure they got the bill. She ranted and raved at Mark's mother for a few more minutes then slammed the phone down.

From beneath my ice packs, I marveled at the sight of my mother getting so upset. She was one of the sweetest ladies and I could count on one hand the number of times I had ever seen her lose her temper. I wondered if any of this anger was going to come my way. It did.

She sat down next to me on the couch and began to clean the wound over my eye. Then, she began to lecture me. "This has got to stop young lady," she said sternly. "You cannot go around fighting everyone who bothers you. Like today, you're going to run into someone bigger and stronger than you and you're going to get seriously hurt. Besides, you're getting to be a young lady now and it's time you started acting like one." She finished cleaning up the gash in my head and decided that I didn't need stitches. "Think about what I said."

It might have surprised her to know that I did think about what she said. Up until now, it didn't occur to me that I could lose a fight. I had taken a few shots from some of the girls I fought but nothing like the pounding Mark had given me. I really thought I was a bad ass. It was the façade I hid behind. Now, Mark had exposed a weakness. I could be taken down for the count. I also knew that it wasn't very ladylike to fight but I figured it wasn't very ladylike to have a harelip either.

Did this mean I was going to have to start ignoring the kids who were picking on me? I wasn't sure I was ready for that. On one hand, I didn't want them to think they could pick on me, but on the other hand, I didn't want to wind up in this condition or worse. I did have some things to think about.

About forty-five minutes had passed with me icing my eyes and Mom starting to make supper, when the doorbell rang. My mom answered it and there stood Mark and a giant of a man beside him.

The big man said, "Sorry to bother you, I'm Mr. Richards and this is my son Mark. He has something he'd like to say to you."

Marks hair had been neatly combed and his eyes were red and puffy. In a quivering voice he said, "I'm the boy who beat up Amy and I'm very sorry."

My mom told him she appreciated the apology.

"He also has something to say to Amy," Mark's father added.

My mom stepped aside and said, "Please come in and sit down."

His dad said, "He won't sit down because he can't sit down."

I giggled a little at this, but my mom shot me a look that said I wouldn't be able to sit down either if I kept it up.

Mark walked over to where I was sitting and said, "I'm sorry Amy, I don't know why I picked on you, but it won't happen again."

A million responses ran through my head but judging from his red eyes and the sheer size of his father, I knew he must have gotten his butt blistered pretty good. Not to mention my mother was glaring at me to respond properly. I decided to call it a draw. "That's okay Mark, no hard feelings."

Our parents chatted for a few more minutes. Then Mark and his father left.

My mom asked me what I thought of all of this. What I thought was that if my father were the size of a lumberjack, I would avoid pissing him off at all costs. What I said was that I actually felt sorry for Mark. My mother pronounced the Richards to be good people who knew how to raise their kids and went back to making supper.

When my father got home from work, he looked at me and said, "You dropped your hands" and after a closer look added, "Twice."

Mom told him what happened and ended by sarcastically suggesting that he just buy me a gun so I could shoot anyone who gave me a hard time. My dad conceded her point and he and I had a long conversation after supper.

He told me he taught me how to box so I could defend myself in grade school. It was only a way to give me some breathing room until I could make friends and get on steady ground emotionally. We discussed that there were still people who were going to tease me, but I had to learn to turn and walk away from them.

By now, the gash in my head was throbbing and my eyes were turning purple, so I told him I understood what he was saying. When he knew my mom was no longer listening, he added, not to worry about losing the fight. My opponent was taller and had a longer reach.

There are two things that are interesting about this story. One, it was a turning point in my life. It was time for me to grow up. So, I retired my boxing gloves. Two, Mark and I both still live near the town we grew up in. I run into him from time to time and he has become one of the sweetest men I have ever met. He never fails to ask about my family and it's easy to see that his kids absolutely adore him.

We were chatting in a gas station not long ago and my mind wandered back to that young boy standing in my house with his teary eyes and his sore backside and my mom saying the Richards were good people who knew how to raise their kids. It appears she was right.

Chapter Six
I Was No Angel Myself

I'll be honest with you, beating the hell out of kids who bullied me did work for a while. Someone would make fun of my face, and the fight was on. After two or three fights, people started leaving me alone. I guess they figured a few minutes of teasing me wasn't worth getting the hell beat out of them. I had a group of close friends that I hung out with and was content with that.

Unfortunately, I developed a bit of a reputation as a bully myself. The chip on my shoulder was so big that if you looked at me wrong, I was ready to pounce. Being a kid myself, I did sometimes tease other kids.

One of the worst spankings I ever got in my life, happened because I was teasing a young, retarded, boy who lived down the street. A group of us were hanging out on the street corner in front of Richie the Retard's, as he was referred to, house. He came outside to join us when someone in the group decided to mimic and tease him. We formed a circle around him and started pushing him back and forth between us.

You would have thought I would have known better. I had been the one in his shoes on many occasions. Where was my understanding and compassion for this young man. I knew while I was standing there joining in this fiasco that I shouldn't have been doing it. I only wanted to fit in with the crowd. Besides, he really didn't seem to understand what we were saying to him.

Unfortunately, his mother was watching from the doorway and understood every word. She came flying out of the house screaming at us. We took off running but not before she got a good look at us and proceeded to walk the neighborhood until she found most of our parents.

When I heard my father call me home a few minutes later, I knew I was in big trouble. I walked into the house to find him standing in the middle of the living room holding a ping pong paddle in his hand.

"Were you in the group of kids that was making fun of Richie?" he asked.

Having no way out of it I admitted I was. Without another word, he put me over his knee and paddled the daylights out of me then sent me to my room. My father almost never hit me, so I understood I had really screwed up.

He left me crying in my room for a bit then came in to talk to me. He told me how disappointed he was that I would take part in something like this. Somehow, that hurt a lot worse than the paddle did. Richie could no more help the fact that he was born retarded than I could help having a harelip. I told him I was just going along with the crowd, and I hadn't meant to hurt Richie's feelings.

"I don't want to hear that crap young lady. How many times did you come home crying because the crowd had chosen you to pick on? Try to remember what it felt like to be on the receiving end of the abuse."

I knew he was right and everything he was saying was true. I promised him that I would never do anything like this again. He hugged me and told me some lessons had to be learned the hard way. So, it seems. That Mark Richards and I learned the same lesson in the same painful way. My father might not have been the size of a lumberjack, but trust me, he got his point across loud and clear.

A few days later, I was riding my bike up the street when I saw Richie playing in his front yard. I didn't think he would understand a verbal apology, so I opened my bag of M&M's and shared them with him. He smiled at me and patted me on the shoulder. A thought occurred to me, he didn't see me as a freak, I was a friend.

His mother came out and I started to run away.

"Wait," she called after me.

Reluctantly, I turned to face this woman whom I was sure was going to yell at me. She sat down and explained to me that Richie had Downs Syndrome and that's why he acted the way he did. She patiently answered all my questions and couldn't have been any nicer to me. I asked her if it was okay if I came over to play with Richie sometimes.

"Richie would love that."

As I hopped on my bike and rode away, I realized I had seen bullying from both sides. Neither experience was very pleasant. I thought about how Richie was probably going to be teased quite a bit throughout his life. Maybe I should teach him how to box.

Chapter Seven
An Editorial

It's important to keep in mind that the events I am describing thus far took place fifty plus years ago. The world was a very different place back then. When we fought, we used our fists, nothing more. Parents didn't sue each other over our childhood battles. They were dealt with over the phone or over a cup of coffee. If we misbehaved, our parents would take a belt or paddle and crack our backsides without fear of going to jail. Things are very different now.

The thought of taking a gun to school never crossed my mind. Even if it had, I wouldn't have known how to get one. I didn't have the internet to teach me how to make a bomb out of Windex and Cool Whip. The whole idea of killing one of my teachers or classmates was absurd. Sadly, it has become a real possibility now.

I watched the Columbine shootings with a mixture of horror and sadness. It was an ugly example of the deadly consequences that can occur when students feel like misfits or outcasts. If we learned nothing more from this tragic event, I hope we learned the importance of inclusion and diversity. I know it's not a cure-all for all the troubled kids out there, but I think it's a step in the right direction.

With all due respect to my father, if my child were born with a cleft lip and palate today, I would never teach her to box. I wound up with a couple of black eyes and a cut. Today a child could be shot, knifed, or sued.

I don't profess to have all the answers but this I do know, if a child is bullied long enough, he will eventually lash out. We as parents, teachers, and coaches must do our level best to end the cycle. Don't turn a blind eye if your child is bullied or is a bully himself. Teach by example. No child is born mean, they learn that from modeling our behavior.

Today, parents are between a rock and a hard place. We must protect our children from strangers, but the fallout is that they learn to fear anyone different from them. We must teach our children not to judge someone by the color of their skin, physical imperfections, etc. I think the best lesson to teach is the golden rule. Do unto others as you'd have done to you. Maybe it really is that simple.

Chapter Eight
The Contest

Growing up meant at least one facet of my life had to change. My days of simply belting anyone who pissed me off were over. Besides, there wasn't always a clear target to unload my anger on.

One example of this was The Contest. I was sitting in study hall bored to death one afternoon. My homework was done, and we weren't allowed to talk so I just sat there looking around. Apparently, someone else was as bored as I was. I noticed some kids were passing around a piece of construction paper and after reading it, would look my way and laugh. I couldn't imagine what was on that paper.

It finally made its way to my table and after a few snickers, the boy next to me laid it down in front of me. The paper was green and in black magic marker someone had announced The Contest for the upcoming sock hop dance. First prize was a date with Sue Conner, a pretty, popular, cheerleader. The booby prize was, you guessed it, a date with me. I looked up to find nearly half the kids in study hall were staring at me to see my reaction.

"Don't cry," I silently begged myself. I could feel the students holding their breath in anticipation.

I won't lie, it hurt quite a bit. More than any black eye ever could. I raced through my options, I could beat up everyone in the study hall, but with only fifteen minutes left there was a time constraint to overcome. I could rifle through everyone's book bag to see who had green construction paper in them, but that wouldn't work either. I looked at my audience, who continued to stare at me with glee. It came to me like a lightning bolt, don't react at all. Take all the fun out of it for them.

It wasn't easy, I was afraid to move. I wanted to cry with all my heart, but I willed myself not to let it happen. I wouldn't even take a deep breath for fear that my bottom lip would start quivering. As silent and still as a rock, I just sat there while the clocked ticked off the final few minutes of study hall. I could feel my heart pounding in my chest. It took every ounce of willpower I had, but I gave them nothing. When the bell finally rang, I could see the disappointment on their faces. I went to the restroom and locked the stall behind me. I shredded that paper into a million pieces and finally, I let myself cry. I sobbed like never before. I would rather take a beating than to ever live through something like this again. Even as I cried, I felt like I had won a moral victory. They didn't have a funny story to tell about how old Snorkel Nose went nuts in study hall.

Luckily, I had an open period next, so I went to the gym, found a basketball, and starting shooting baskets. This simple act was a way to gain a tremendous amount of respect from my peers.

Chapter Nine
Sports. Everyone Loves a Winner

One of the reasons I didn't become a suicidal, high school dropout was sports. My sister was fifteen years older than me and had gotten married when I was three. My brother-in-law, Bill, became a second father to me. Thanks to him, I could out hit, outshoot, and outrun almost every boy in the neighborhood. He was pitching me curve balls by the time I was six. As a result, I developed some pretty good hand eye coordination.

He would gather as many kids as he could find and divide us into teams. We played football, baseball, and basketball. A strange thing started to happen. I was no longer the girl they tormented; I was the girl they wanted on their team. They would knock on my door to come join their pick-up games. It was the one arena in my life where I didn't feel inferior to anyone.

In the summer before I was to enter high school, I was very worried. The kids in junior high were used to me and I was no longer much of a running joke to them. But high school would bring a bunch of new kids that I never met.

I couldn't help but think I was going to be treated like a freak show attraction again. I dreaded the very thought of entering Jackson High School. Was my first day there going to be as horrible as my first day of junior high?

While reading the newspaper one day that summer, I saw a notice in the sports section about tryouts for volleyball at Jackson High. *Volleyball*, I thought, *what the hell*. I marked the date on the calendar and read everything I could find about the sport. My only experience was playing in the sand at Lake Cable Beach.

On a hot day in August, I walked into the gym at Jackson for the first time. It was huge compared to the gym in junior high. I looked around at the banners and the bleachers and thought, *I love this place*. I counted about twenty-five girls in the gym there to try out for the team. I recognized a few friends from junior high and hung out with them. We were asked to pair off and bump the ball back and forth. I paired off with a girl named Andrea who asked me to be her partner. She would become one of my closest friends throughout high school.

We passed the ball back and forth while the coaches were walking amongst us watching. *Nothing too tough so far*, I thought. Next, we were asked to serve. Having played a little tennis, I was used to hitting a ball over a net and used a similar motion to serve the volleyball.

After a few serves, the coach, a wonderful woman named Fran Bartholomew walked over. She tossed me another ball and asked, "Can you do that again?"

I sent another serve over the net.

"Stay there," she told me. She had a few girls line up on the opposite side of the net and asked me to serve to them. I served a lot of aces, a few into the net, and many they could not return. She walked back over to me and said, "Well done, Laschinske."

I stared at her dumbfounded and thought, *How does she know my name*?

She must have read the confusion on my face because she smiled at me and said, "Your name is on the back of your jersey."

I laughed; I had forgotten what shirt I had on. I left my first day of try-outs elated. I had impressed the coach, and I had made a great new friend in Andrea.

Tryouts lasted about two weeks. Every day I would watch what the older girls were doing and tried to imitate them. My favorite part of the game was spiking the ball. It felt so good to smash the ball to the floor. The older girls, instead of treating me like a freak, gave me pointers on how to improve my technique. I was starting to make new friends before school even started.

On the last day of tryouts, Coach Bartholomew had us all sit in a circle on the floor. She thanked all of us for trying out and said unfortunately, only a few of us would make the team. There was a list of names on the locker room door and only the girls whose names were on it should report to practice after the first day of school. A few of the girls got up and ran to see if they had made the team but I sat frozen on the floor. I wasn't surprised how much this meant to me. This was the first time in my life where I walked into a group of strangers and hadn't been treated like a leper. I know somewhere in my mind; the slide trombone fiasco was replaying itself.

I watched as some of the other girls came back into the gym laughing and fist pumping while others were crying and stomping off. Andrea and I finally made our way over to the list on the door. There were both of our names in black and white. I wanted to weep with relief. I had been accepted and it felt great, and I was delighted that Andrea was going on this journey with me.

I practically danced out to the car where my dad was waiting and told him I made the team. We picked up my mom and went out to dinner to celebrate. I went from dreading the first day of school to hoping it would start soon all because of volleyball. Andrea and I talked, like the teenage girls we were, on the phone about volleyball every day.

School finally started and everything went fine. A few of my new teammates were in some of my classes and that really helped. If anyone was staring at me, I didn't notice because I was so excited about volleyball practice.

After school, I raced to the gym for my first official day of my volleyball career. Coach Bartholomew or Bart, as we came to call her, greeted us there. She opened the practice by having us all sit in the bleachers. She asked us to look around and accept that we were all part of a team now.

Teammates treated each other with respect and helped each other out. She said she would not tolerate any disrespect towards each other or towards her. She said we were a chain now and could not function with a broken link. Then she started practice. I never forgot her words. I loved being part of the team, part of the chain. We hadn't even started yet, but I loved volleyball already.

I would go on to play for Bart for the next three years. I never had so much respect for anyone outside of my family than I did for her. She made me a better volleyball player, I won many awards for my playing abilities, but more importantly, she made me a better person. She fostered a family like environment on her team where I was not only accepted, I developed a few social skills as well. Her office door was always open, and I found I could drop in to talk whenever I needed to.

I think she knew how much being on her team was helping me. It offered me the chance to gain the acceptance I desperately craved and gave me an outlet for all the pent-up anger I still carried with me.

As I developed as an athlete, my confidence and my self-esteem grew. Hearing the fans cheer and chant my name meant the world to me. Bart allowed me to be confident but never cocky. It was heady stuff reading my name in the paper and have people know me as an athlete rather than a freak. But as soon as I decided I was God's gift to the volleyball playing world, Bart would pull me back down to earth.

She threatened to bench me once after one practice where I didn't feel the need to hustle. BENCH ME! The greatest player on the planet. I shot her a look that said, "You wouldn't dare." I could not have been more wrong.

She did bench me for the next game. It was agonizing sitting on the bench watching my teammates lose the first of a best of three match. I wound up still on the bench at the start of the second game.

My buddy Andrea said to me, "Do something, you asshole. Tell her you're sorry, kiss her ass, whatever you need to do to get back on the floor."

Finally went and sat down next to Bart. "I'm sorry," I told her. "I will hustle my butt off from now on."

That must have been what she was looking for because she called a time-out and put me in the game. Shout out to all my teammates who rather than being pissed at me, rallied hard to win the next two games to take the match. One look at Bart however, told me all was not forgiven.

35

After the game, she summoned me to her office and told me to shut the door. She never raised her voice, but she told me in no uncertain terms that she would not put up with this crap from me. I was part of A team not THE team. She said she would rather bench me and lose every game than let me get away with being lazy. Her voice softened a bit, she told me she knew how much playing volleyball meant to me. She knew how much the cheering and the success was helping me. She told me not to take it all for granted. I apologized to her again and promised to do better.

I left her office with my tail between my legs but my respect for her grew. After all this sport had done for me, the least I could do was give it everything I had. I also admired her for not screaming at me. She would have been well within her rights to rip my head off.

A few days later at practice, I dove over a table to keep the ball from going out of bounds.

Bart grinned at me from ear to ear. "Nice hustle," she said.

Chapter Ten
Okay, Not Everyone

It's hard to say what my life would have been like without sports to occupy my time. I'm sure I would have been lonely, most of my friends were teammates from one sport or another. The fact that I was searching for a group where I fit in leads me to believe I could have easily become caught up in drugs or alcohol.

Having a giving, caring coach like Bart really made a difference in my life. She was everything I needed then. Soft and kind, but not afraid to deliver a verbal ass-kicking when I needed it. I could never thank her enough for keeping me on track and out of trouble. I was so fortunate to have her as a mentor.

I marked the passing of my high school years not by classes or semesters but by seasons. Volleyball in the fall, basketball in the winter, and track in the spring. I enjoyed a measure of success in each sport I played. My father beamed with pride every time he opened the sports section of the newspaper and found my name in some article. Very slowly, I began to overcome the crippling shyness I suffered from. When people did stare at me, I liked to pretend it was because they recognized me from a picture in the paper instead of my harelip. Sports was the one area that I didn't mind having the spotlight on me. That isn't to say that it was all smooth sailing.

Of all the sports I played, I was wild about basketball. I loved the fact that your opponent wasn't on the other side of a net but was right there in your face. The bad side was that trash-talking was a real thing and was not very nice.

As naturally as volleyball had come to me, I really had to work at basketball. Every day I worked on my shooting and rebounding and became proficient enough to make the team. Then there was the coach.

Candy Evans was the anti-Bart of coaching. A brash, young woman that had a swagger about her that intimidated the hell out of me. She yelled loudly and often, and I was convinced from the start that she hated me. She did nothing to dispute this notion. She saw that I had a chip on my shoulder, but where Bart would gently coax it off, Candy tried to knock it off with a sledgehammer. We clashed like oil and water over almost everything. It was the epitome of a love/hate relationship.

Every day, she would scream at me or taunt me at practice, and I would smart mouth her back. Then she would send me running around the gym for punishment laps. By the end of my career, I was in the best shape of my life. I learned how truly stubborn I can be. I told my dad after every practice, "Evans hates me."

He replied, "She's just trying to toughen you up."

I had my doubts.

I will say this for her, she taught me everything I know about basketball. Her knowledge of the game was very impressive. I will also say this for her, she never accepted self-pity from me. Not long into my first season, an opposing player made a crack about my face. I immediately threw a wicked elbow right into the middle of her chest. I was of course hit with a technical foul. The opposing fans then started taunting me from the bleachers.

Completely enraged, I stood in front of them and yelled, "You can all fuck off."

Evans called for a sub and pulled me out of the game. I was livid.

When I reached the bench, she grabbed me by the front of my jersey and yelled, "What the hell are you doing?"

Our eyes locked for a moment before mine started welling up with tears. "I've put up with as much bullshit about my face as I can stand," I choked out.

I knew in an instant that she didn't hate me. The look that crossed her face just then was so compassionate and understanding. I had caught a glimpse of what was underneath that tough exterior. She and I were basically two of a kind. Her eyes were tearing up and she tried to speak but couldn't.

To cover this rare display of humanity, she yelled at me, "Sit your ass down, we'll talk later."

The next day at practice, she walked over to me and put her arm around my shoulder. "Come with me," she said and led me into the locker room.

The whole gym went silent and I'm sure everyone was thinking, "Evans is going to kill her."

We had a chat about what happened. She was so sweet and caring about understanding what I was going through, she told me she knew it was rough. Then she went into full Evans mode when talking about my handling of the situation. She yelled at me for fifteen solid minutes about elbowing the other girl, the technical foul and of course, yelling profanities at the opposing fans. She finished by telling me she needs me in the game, not on the bench. "Let your play speak for you and shut that damn mouth of yours." Then she did something that shocked me, she hugged me. "Let's get back to practice."

We would continue having our battles over the years, including one where we damn near came to blows in the locker room, but I never felt like she hated me anymore. It took me years to fully understand the lessons she was trying to teach me. I realized as I got older, that she was the first person not to melt with pity over my face. It was simply not an option with her. She held me accountable for my actions on and off the court. I didn't like it then, but I appreciate it now. Just like Bart, Candy Evans became an important part in my becoming the person I am today, and I thank her for that.

My track coach, Neitz, was the coolest guy on the planet. He knew from the start that I really wanted to play softball in the spring, but he told me if I joined the track team, he would basically let me do what I wanted, and he was true to his word.

I showed up at the meets, threw the shot put and discus, won most of the time, then went home. The only time he ever said anything to me was when the security guard at school caught me smoking in my car on the way out of the school parking lot. Neitz called me over and asked me to wait until I was off school property to light up. I adored him. He let me, do me.

Chapter Eleven
Keith

Sports did wonders for my confidence and self-esteem. Put a volleyball or basketball in my hands and I lost all signs of shyness. I was in my element on the court. The problems started the minute I left the gym.

In the classroom, I reverted to the shy, misfit, of my youth. I rarely spoke to anyone and when I did, I had a habit of putting my hands in front of my face in an attempt to hide my harelip. I never raised my hand in class even if I knew the answer because the thought of everybody looking at me when I spoke terrified me.

I was happiest when everyone ignored me. The same girl who could tear you up on the court, couldn't look you in the eye off it. I tried to pretend it didn't bother me to be this way. I tried to pretend that it didn't matter that I didn't go on dates or receive any valentines. I could pretend all I wanted but the fact remains that it did bother me more than I would ever admit.

On Sweethearts Day, the cheerleaders would sell flowers to the boys to give to their sweethearts. Different colored roses signified different things. Red meant love, yellow meant friendship, and orange meant you had a secret admirer. The cheerleaders would go around from class to class passing out these flowers.

Every time they entered one of my classrooms, I secretly hoped I would get one. I never did. The funny thing about the boys I knew was the only time they wanted anything to do with me was if they needed a third baseman.

So, I watched in envy as the other girls collected their flowers and pinned them on their shirts. I had dozens of trophies at home, but I would have traded them all for one of those flowers. I resigned myself that having a harelip and romance did not go together. Janis Ian was right; love was meant for beauty queens.

All of this changed during my sophomore year. My second period class was Spanish, and I hated it. Apparently, the boy who sat behind me hated it too. He paid absolutely no attention during class and was always getting yelled at. I would find myself at my desk giggling wildly at his antics. One day, he tapped me on the shoulder and asked for a piece of paper. I tore a page out of my notebook and handed it to him. He was a handsome devil I noticed, with dark hair and dark eyes.

He tapped me on the shoulder again and passed the paper back to me. On it, he had written, "Have you seen Helen Keller's new boyfriend?"

I shook my head no.

"Neither has she," he said and then laughed hysterically.

I laughed out loud until the teacher turned to us and said, "Hey you two, knock it off."

I turned around and was horrified to find all eyes exactly where I didn't want them to be, on me. I turned beet red and stared at my desk until she went on with the lesson. Behind me, I could hear Keith snickering at his joke. He passed me another piece of paper, "Sorry," it said.

I began to look forward to Spanish class. He talked

to me every day although I never uttered more than a few words to him. Second period was when they did the announcements over the loudspeaker.

Every time they said my name for scoring the most points or winning the shot put, he would stand up and cheer wildly while clapping me on the back, "Way to go Champ."

Soon he had the whole class joining him. I was both flattered and dumbfounded by his interest in me. I was also beginning to have a serious crush on him. I told myself that there was no way this cute, funny, boy would ever look twice at someone like me. As handsome as he was, I was sure he could have his pick of any girl in the school and he sure as hell wasn't going to pick me.

One day, right before class, he asked me if I liked Mexican food.

"Yes," I replied.

"Would you like to have dinner with me on Friday night?"

I stared at him completely speechless. I think I was waiting for the punchline. Did he just ask me out on a date? I heard him with my own ears, but I couldn't convince my heart he did.

"Okay," I heard myself say.

He had me write my address and phone number down and I watched him fold it up and slip it in his pocket.

Concentrating on the lesson was out of the question. A date! This guy had just asked me out on a date. There must be some mistake. Cute boys do not go on dates with ugly girls with harelips. It just didn't happen.

Try not to get too excited, I begged myself. *It's only Tuesday and he has plenty of time to change his mind.*

Wednesday and Thursday passed with no mention of cancelling our date. I hadn't told anyone, not even my parents, to save myself the humiliation when Keith came to his senses and told me to forget it. On Friday, he told me he would pick me up at six. As unbelievable as it was, it looked like I was going on a date.

Chapter Twelve
The Date

I walked in the door Friday after school ready to have a nervous breakdown. What was I going to wear? What were we going to talk about? What if he hates me? What if I trip and fall on my way into the restaurant? What if my mom doesn't let me go? I hadn't asked her permission to go just in case it never happened. I knew she suffered right along with me whenever I came home crying from yet another humiliating experience. I was so sure Keith was going to back out of this date that I never even mentioned it to her, but now he was due to pick me up in two hours.

Mom was in the kitchen starting supper when I walked into the house. As casually as I could manage, I said, "Don't set a place for me, if it's alright with you, I have a date tonight."

She turned to me and said, "A date, honey that's wonderful. With who?"

I forgot all about trying to keep it casual. I babbled out the whole story about the cute, funny, boy in my Spanish class. I strategically omitted the part about the teacher yelling at us to pay attention. As she was listening, she was getting as excited as I was. Soon, we were carrying on like two schoolgirls. My father was a different matter.

My father had suffered a major stroke my freshmen

year and it had robbed him of most of his ability to speak clearly. He never said more than a few words at a time. He did, however, remain a proud man who was a little too overprotective of me.

Upon hearing I had a date, he said two words, "Meet him."

I knew what he meant. Before he would agree to let me go, Keith was going to have to come in to meet him. My dad was a great guy and he and I had an uncanny ability to communicate non-verbally, but how would Keith react to this.

I hurried to shower and dress for my date. Every time the phone rang, I was sure it was Keith calling to cancel. My mind would still not fully accept that he was willingly taking me out. Was he really going to be seen in public with me? It had to be a joke I decided. He was going to take me to a restaurant where all his buddies were waiting to make fun of me. Maybe he lost a bet. By the time I finished getting ready, I was sure this was the case.

Promptly at six, I heard a car pull into the driveway. I peeked out my bedroom window and watched Keith step out of a beautiful Mustang. *He is so good looking*, I thought, *there must be a catch here somewhere*. I walked out and answered the doorbell.

"Hi," he said. "You look great."

I smiled shyly at him. "Please come in and meet my folks."

He walked into the house and told me that his mom and my sister were good friends.

So that's it, I thought, *my sister got his mom to make him ask me out.*

I introduced him to my mom and that exchange was very pleasant. Now for the moment I was dreading.

"This is my dad." He stepped forward and shook my father's hand.

"Pleased to meet you sir."

I knew my dad liked this show of respect on Keith's part by the look on his face. Then, Keith said exactly the right thing, "What time would you like me to have Amy home by."

My dad tapped his watch, and I told Keith my curfew was eleven. Keith watched this exchange with a slightly puzzled look on his face. I explained about my dad's stroke and Keith nodded and promised to have me home on time. We said our good-byes and headed out the door.

He held my car door open for me and as he walked around the car to get in, I couldn't stand it anymore.

"Look," I said, "if your mother made you ask me out, we can call this off and I'll understand."

He looked at me blankly.

I continued, "If this is some sort of joke or dare, please tell me up front."

I wanted to believe so badly that he was here of his own free will, but I had been the punchline of these scenarios' way too often. I made myself look into his eyes. I could tell he really didn't understand what I was talking about.

Now I was making a complete ass out of myself, and we hadn't even pulled out of the driveway yet. "I just thought there was some reason you asked me out," I finished meekly.

"There is," he replied. "I like you.

We drove to the restaurant making small talk. He told me I had met him and his twin brother before when we were little kids at my sister's house. I remembered

47

his family coming over to swim. I found myself relaxing in spite of myself.

When we arrived at the restaurant with no evil fanfare awaiting me. I really started to enjoy myself. He had a wickedly funny sense of humor, and my sides hurt from laughing. He asked me if I had seen their new menu.

When I replied, "No, neither has Helen Keller," I thought he was going to spit his drink out all over the place.

Emboldened by my little joke, I became more comfortable by the minute. You could even say I was chatty. I laughed more sitting there with him than I had in my entire life. I was amazed when he checked his watch and said it was after ten. We had been sitting there for hours.

When we pulled into my driveway, he said, "My brother is throwing a party at Sippo Lake tomorrow night, wanna go?"

This was almost too good to be true. Our first date was barely over, and he was already asking for a second.

"Sure," I replied.

"Great, I'll call you tomorrow and we'll set it up." He got out and walked around to let me out. Just then, the porch lights flicked on and off. Keith laughed and said, "It must be eleven." He got back in his car. "See ya tomorrow."

I floated up the walk and into the house. My father tapped his watch and gave me a thumbs up sign. My mother was watching me intently and asked a little too quickly how it went.

"It went great," I told her.

Relief spread across her face, and she beamed at me. She turned away but not before I caught the single tear that ran down her cheek.

She had been every bit as worried about this date as me. I asked their permission to go to the party tomorrow night then I kissed them both and went to bed. Sleep was a long time coming.

I lay awake for hours pondering the events of the evening. How did he do that? How did he get me out on a date? How did he get me to talk like that? What was it about him that let me open up that way? Does he really like me? He must or else why would he invite me to his brother's party? God is he cute. Why would he be interested in me? Questions swirled around in my head. I finally fell asleep happier than I had ever been.

Chapter Thirteen
Laughter Really is the Best Medicine

Saturday evening, Keith showed up at my house to pick me up for the party. I was excited but worried. Last night was wonderful but that was just he and I. Tonight, there was going to be a whole bunch of people I didn't know. That nagging feeling that I was going to be the punchline of some evil prank crept back into my head. Was last night just a set up for something awful tonight? I looked for any signs from Keith that this was the case, but he was just as funny and nice as he was the night before.

We drove to Sippo Lake to a clearing in the trees. There were about thirty kids there, most of whom I recognized from school. Everyone was friendly and I started to let myself relax. One girl, Julie, I knew only by her reputation as a party girl. I discovered that it was true. Julie could party so hard that she could put some rock bands to shame. There was some beer and pot at the party, and I could tell Julie had sampled both. A roaring bonfire had been built and I sat between Julie and Keith. Between the two of them, I laughed so hard I couldn't breathe.

Like Keith, she found anything and everything funny. I did notice that she was never cruel. She teased people but in a lighthearted, airy manner. Everyone loved her. We all drank, smoked, and danced for hours. I was having the time of my life.

Suddenly, Keith's brother Chris yelled, "Is everyone ready to go skinny-dipping?"

Everyone began to cheer and yell and seemed to be up for it. Everyone but me. Although I was plied with a little booze and weed, I was not ready to party naked with these people. It was only my second date with Keith, and I didn't know most of these kids.

"Everyone! Go in the woods, take off your clothes, and on the count of three, run and jump in the lake," Chris instructed the crowd.

Keith took me by the hand and was leading me towards the woods.

"Wait a minute, Keith," I stammered. "I'm not ready to…"

He cut me off. "Don't worry, we aren't doing this, follow me." We went in the woods, remained clothed, and he said, "Just watch."

On the count of three, Julie, and only Julie, ran down the hill stark naked and screaming. I watched in horrified fascination as she disappeared beneath the surface of the water. When she resurfaced, she looked around and realizing that she was the sole skinny dipper, threw her head backed and roared with laughter.

I was stunned.

I would still be doing my life sentence for murdering Chris. Everyone emerged from the woods dying with laughter, but no one was laughing harder than Julie. Someone handed her a blanket as she walked out of the lake, and she took her seat beside me again. I was staring at her in complete admiration. She taught me such a valuable lesson right then and there and gave me a coping tool that I would use for the rest of my life. Laughter.

Keith was teaching me the power of humor, but Julie taught me the power in laughing at yourself. She could dish it out for sure, but as I had just witnessed, she could damn well take it too. She turned to me and said, "Wasn't that awesome?"

I asked, "Can I ask you something? Didn't that piss you off at all?"

She looked at me for a moment then replied, "No, it was all in good fun."

I decided right then and there that she was the coolest person I had ever met. I think of her from time to time whenever I can turn myself into the punchline. Laugh at yourself then others won't have to.

Chapter Fourteen
Marsha Plants a Seed

My sister Marsha was fifteen and my brother thirteen when I was born. I think it's safe to assume that I was not a planned pregnancy. Unfortunately, my brother Mark died when I was four so my memories of him are hazy, but my sister and I were very close despite the age difference.

She was often mistaken for my mother and in many ways, she was a second mother to me. When she got her first paycheck, she bought me a swing set with it. Through the years I found that I could talk to her about anything and could always depend on her to be honest with me.

Marsha was a beautiful woman with clear, blue eyes, and a heart of gold. She possessed a quick wit and a sense of humor that got me through some of the toughest times of my life. She married her husband Bill when I was three and although we didn't grow up together, I spent many days at her house. She gave me my love of music. We would spend hours listening to records, Elvis, Linda Ronstadt, the Beach Boys, to name a few. It was my safe space.

One night when I was around seventeen, she called me and asked me to come over and watch some television with her. This wasn't unusual as we often got pizza and watched movies together.

We fixed our plates and settled into the living room when I said, "What are we watching?"

She looked at me with a somewhat odd look on her face and said, "The Body Human."

I laughed at her and said, "If this is a show about sex, or babies being born, I already had this talk with mom."

She never even cracked a smile. "No," she replied, "It's about something else."

The show came on and set in motion a chain of events that would change my life forever.

The show was about plastic surgery. There was this poor woman on it that had the biggest nose of any human I had ever seen before. It was so big; it gave her the appearance of being cross-eyed. She talked about how she was teased unmercifully about her nose, so she decided to seek help from a plastic surgeon.

I listened in complete fascination as the doctor described how he was going to break her nose, file the excess bone off, and leave her with a normal sized nose. They showed the actual surgery, and I was okay with all of it until the doctor took a hammer and chisel and cracked her nose to break it. I winced a bit at this.

He had peeled her face back from her hairline and when he was done, pulled her face back up and stitched it up in her hairline to hide the scars. When they showed her again, she was bandaged from the top of her head to her chin with two eyes and a mouth hole. At that point I though there's no way I would do that. Then they showed her a few months later and the transformation was incredible. Her nose looked very normal and there were no visible scars. I began to toy with the idea that maybe there was something that could be done to improve my appearance.

When the show was over, Marsha was unusually quiet. Every time I glanced her way, I noticed that she was staring at me intently. It was like she was willing me to read her mind. We had never had any deep conversation about my harelip and cleft palate or my physical appearance.

I finally turned to face her and asked, "Do you think they could do anything to help me?"

She jumped up from her chair and flung her arms around my neck and hugged me tightly. Then, she burst into tears. She said if I wanted her to, she would make some calls to gather some information on the subject.

"Why are you crying?" I asked her.

She said that she had wanted to suggest something like this for a long time, but she wanted it to be my idea. She made it perfectly clear that it didn't matter to her if I decided not to do anything, but she would be glad to help me through it if I did.

A week or two later she came over to the house and said she had found a surgeon in Akron who specialized in cleft lip and palate reconstruction. We sat down and discussed the idea with our parents. They had some reservations about the whole thing but ultimately decided it was up to me.

I figured it couldn't hurt to go talk with this doctor, so I agreed to make an appointment. Three weeks later I was off to meet Dr. James Lehman.

Chapter Fifteen
Dr. Lehman

The day of my appointment with Dr. Lehman finally arrived. I greeted it with a mixture of hope and dread. I tried to imagine what I would look like after surgery but couldn't do it. I also tried not to think of him breaking my nose with a hammer.

I was extremely nervous about going under the knife. My mom told me I had several surgeries as a baby, in fact, I had spent the first two years of my life in and out of the hospital but of course I had no memory of it. Driving to the Dr.'s office, the three of us were unusually quiet, all of us lost in our own thoughts.

Upon arrival, I was checked in and soon escorted to an exam room with my mom and sister in tow. Dr. Lehman entered the room and greeted us all very warmly. Then things turned very weird. He pulled up a chair right in front of me, took out a sketch pad, and stared directly into my face. Every now and again, he would reach out and touch my nose or lips, then go back to drawing. I felt so awkward and stupid while trying to look anywhere but at him.

At one point, he pulled out my bottom lip and pinched it. I glanced at my sister and we both started laughing. Dr. Lehman laughed and explained that he was just seeing how much tissue I had on my bottom lip.

He took out a small tape measure and measured the length of my nose and the distance between my eyes, then he would jot some notes down on his sketch pad. It all had a probed by an alien vibe to it.

When he finished, he showed us the sketch pad with the picture he had drawn. I looked at it in awe. He explained to us all the things he wanted to do. First, he would break my nose and reshape and straighten it up a bit.

Because of the cleft palate, my right eye didn't open as wide as my left. His plan was to remove a small flap of skin from my eyelid to give it the appearance that it was open wider. Finally, if there was enough tissue in my bottom lip, he would remove it and form a top lip where there was now just a thin line. I listened to all of this in wonder. I would have had the surgery right then until my sister asked her first question.

"What if she doesn't have enough tissue in her bottom lip."

"No problem," he answered. "I'll do a procedure where I harvest the tissue from her vagina."

WHAT! You want to take a piece of my VAGINA and put it on my FACE. Oh, hell no, my mind screamed.

All three of us gaped at him like he had suddenly started speaking Greek.

He explained that the tissue in your vagina was the same as the tissue of the lips on your face and no one would be able to tell the difference. I almost jumped off the table and headed out the door. Imagine yourself at seventeen trying to process this gem. I didn't hear too much more of what he said because my mind couldn't get past the vagina thing. The only other thought I had was ABSOLUTELY NOT. I heard my mom tell him that we had a lot to talk about and she would call the office and let him know what we decided.

When we got back to the car, I announced that there was no way any of this was going to happened. We weren't going to talk about it, think about it, or even mention it ever again. If anyone in this car mentioned vagina harvesting, I was getting out and walking home. I sat in stony silence all the way home. Hope and expectations can be a double-edged sword. Exhilarating when they work out and crushing when they don't.

I knew my sister well enough to know that this wasn't over. She and I didn't share many family traits. We didn't look alike, she was very smart, and she had no athletic ability whatsoever.

But the one trait we did share was stubbornness. If either one of us dug our heals in, look out. Marsha was also in nursing school so that qualified her, in our family, as the authority on all things medical. She did, however, have the good sense to wait a few days before broaching the subject again.

She strolled into the house a few days later and set out to change my mind. Our parents cleared out of the basement like rats on a sinking ship. They knew a battle of epic proportions was about to take place. I decided to draw first blood. "I know why you're here and you're wasting your damn time. I'm not going through with this."

She glared at me and responded, "You're acting like a spoiled little bitch."

What ensued, was an argument that featured must swearing, a little shoving, and silent stand-offs when we were both too angry to speak. It got so bad that at one point, my mom yelled down that she was going to wash our mouths out with soap if we didn't stop all the cussing.

Even in the heat of battle, the image of my mom washing my thirty-two-year-old sister's mouth out made me laugh. The timing was perfect. We both got to giggling and the anger went away.

"Look," Marsha said, "you are many things, but no one could every call you a chicken. Don't let this whole vagina thing stop you from doing this." Then my very wise sister slammed the door on any argument I could muster. "He might not need any extra tissue and if he does, no one will know where it came from unless you tell them."

I took a deep breath. Sensing victory, Marsha walked over to hug me.

"Okay, I'll have the surgery."

Marsha held me for a long time and told me she was proud of me.

Then she yelled, "Mom, Amy keeps cussing."

Chapter Sixteen
The Surgery

I can't remember the exact date, but I checked into Akron Children's Hospital on Monday afternoon. To say I was scared would be the understatement of the century. I was petrified. Until now, the only hospital visits I could remember were a few trips to the ER for some stitches and a broken hand.

I was trying to keep a brave face for my mother who was also a nervous wreck. My poor mother suffered just as much, if not more, than I did throughout the years. I knew every time I came home crying from the latest drama concerning my face, it broke her heart.

She would dry my tears, clean my wounds. and console her baby girl as best she could. We had talked a little about my upcoming operation but in truth, neither of us knew quite what to expect. I had my pre-op blood tests and x-rays done then settled into my room.

Dr. Lehman came in and went over all the things he had planned to do. When he mentioned vaginal tissue again, I had to fight the urge to get dressed and bolt from the room. He turned to my mom and said, "Now mother, she's going to look a whole lot worse before she looks better. She'll be swollen and bloody with black eyes. I just want you to be prepared for that."

My mom nodded at him, but I knew she was going to be a mess. In many ways, this was going to be easier on me than it would on her. Fortunately, my sister would be joining us tomorrow morning so mom wouldn't have to deal with this alone. A nurse came in with consent forms and I noticed my mother's hand trembled slightly as she signed them. It was getting late, so my mom left for her hotel room. She bent down to kiss me as we both fought back tears. I didn't think either one of us was going to get much sleep.

After she left, alone in my room, I completely fell apart. Worry and panic started to set in. Was I making a huge mistake? What if the surgery got botched and I wound up looking even worse? What if I died on the table putting my parents through the loss of another child? And the whole vagina tissue issue made me want to throw up. I wondered if it was too late to call the whole thing off. A wonderful nurse entered my room and could see that I was on the verge of a nervous breakdown.

She hugged me and tried to assure me that everything was going to be alright. Then she said, "I'll be right back with my magic pills, and I promise you, you'll feel better."

Magic pills? What the hell was she talking about? She came back in with two pills for me to take and after I swallowed them, said, "Goodnight."

I lay there for a bit then I started to feel much better. *God bless those magic pills*, I thought. I entered a dream like state and all my worries melted away. Soon, I was singing to myself. "You ain't nothing but a hound dog, crying all the time."

The nurse returned and played the air guitar to accompany my vocals. She also filled the role of back-up singer. Multi-talented, this girl. That was the last thing I remembered before drifting off to sleep.

Bright and early the next morning, I awoke to find my mom and sister standing by my bedside. I started to tell them about my impromptu concert appearance the night before.

My sister laughed and said, "Aren't sedatives great?"

When the orderly entered the room to transport me to the operating room, I couldn't help but tear up again.

The panic was coming back. My mom turned to stare out the window to hide her own tears and my sister leaned down and whispered in my ear, "You fucking got this Elvis."

The first thing I noticed was that it was freezing in the OR. A bunch of nurses were flitting about the room doing things. One strapped me down to the table with my arms stretched out in a sort of Jesus pose. Another wheeled in a tray full of the instruments for the doctor.

Even though it was covered, I could clearly make out the shape of the nose breaking hammer underneath.

LOOK SOMEWHERE ELSE, my brain cried.

The Anesthesiologist came in and started an IV. He said he was going to start some medicine to help me relax. After a few minutes, I couldn't have cared less what they were doing. Dr. Lehman came in and asked me if I was ready.

"Sure thing, Doc," I answered him.

More medicine was added to my IV and a mask was placed over my nose and mouth. I was instructed to count backward from ten, then nothing but blackness.

When I came to, I was in a different room hooked up to all kinds of tubes and monitors. I could hear a nurse telling me to open my eyes, but I was still sleepy, so I kept drifting off. She kept getting louder and bitchier until I finally woke up.

I tried to ask her a question but discovered I couldn't move my lips.

"Don't try to talk," said her bitchy self. "Your lips are sewn shut."

I ran my tongue along the inside of my lips and discovered she was right. I also noticed that I had two rubber tubes in both corners of my mouth so I could breathe.

I was frustrated because I had a very important question to ask but couldn't. Soon, another orderly took me back to my room. I was wondering why I wasn't in any pain. That, I discovered, would come later.

My mom and sister came back into my room, and I must have looked terrible because they both burst out in tears. My mom bent down and was stroking my arm gently. I tried to ask her my question, but she couldn't make out what I was trying to say. Marsha grabbed a piece of paper from her purse.

"Vagina?" I wrote.

She told me no, there had been enough tissue in my bottom lip. My vagina was intact and where it belonged, and my face remained vaginaless. I could have cried. I wrote that I was not in any pain, just tired.

They both kissed me and said they would be back tomorrow. I grabbed my mom's hand and held on a minute.

"Go home, get some sleep, I'm okay," I wrote. "Love you both."

Chapter Seventeen
There's the Pain

I woke up at some point in the middle of the night and thought, "Someone has repeatedly struck me in the face with a large, blunt, object."

The pain was incredible. My nose had indeed been broken and was packed with gauze. My eyes were so swollen, I could barely open them. There was a burning sensation in my eyelid that was driving me insane.

Luckily, my lips were still numb, but they felt heavy like they were made from modeling clay (better than a piece of my vagina) but still very uncomfortable. I was in agony. To complete my misery, I had a splitting headache. I fumbled for the call button to summon a nurse. Had I just made the biggest mistake of my young life?

I heard someone singing in the hallway. "Return to sender, address unknown."

Great, I thought, *I am either suffering from a seizure or was brain damaged from the operation*. My favorite nurse/back-up singer from the night before entered the room.

She said, "I'm just guessing here, but I bet you want something for the pain."

I nodded my head yes and wrote on my paper, "Magic pills?"

"Oh no my dear, tonight you will get magic morphine. Hang tight a sec." She returned with a shot and after giving it to me, sat down on the edge of my bed.

She took a cool towel and laid it across my forehead. Then she patted my hand until I began to drift back to sleep. I remember thinking, "She's not a nurse, she's an angel."

A few hours later, I awoke to the pain starting again and I really had to pee. I pushed the call light, and my favorite nurse came back in. "Pee," I wrote on my paper.

"Okay baby, let me help you out of bed." She led me to the bathroom and turned on the light.

I saw my reflection in the mirror and almost peed on the floor. No wonder my mom and sister had gotten so emotional when they saw me. I was bandaged like a mummy, but you could see my eyes were just purple slits and the bandages had blood all over them.

"Fuck," I muttered. That came out pretty clear.

"I know kiddo," said my nurse.

When I finished, she helped me back to bed. Before I could think about how bad I looked, it was magic morphine time again.

The next day my family returned to find me staring at a bowl of split-pea soup. One of the tubes and been removed from the corner of my mouth and they actually thought I was going to suck this shit into my mouth.

My mom tried to get me to eat it by saying I needed to keep up my strength.

Not that bad, I thought, *I rather starve*.

Dr. Lehman came in to check on me and when he looked at the bowl of green, slimy soup, asked,

"There's not much chance you're going to eat that is there?"

I shook my head no.

"How about some chicken broth?" he asked.

Now he was speaking my language.

A new bowl of soup was brought to my room, then the adventure began. Try sucking anything through a straw when you can't feel your lips. I spilled the soup all over myself and only managed to get a few drops in my mouth. This time, it was my mom to the rescue.

She dipped the straw into the broth, covered the top with her finger, then placed the straw in my mouth and released her finger. Watching her, I couldn't help but laugh. Although I couldn't open my mouth, and I was not a baby. Her mouth would open wide with every spoonful. I continued to let her feed me this way because I knew it made her feel helpful.

I stayed in the hospital for a few more days until Dr. Lehman came in and asked me if I was ready to go home.

"Hell yes!"

He released me with some prescriptions and an appointment to return to his office in two weeks to remove the stitches. I was to maintain an all-liquid diet until then.

I left a note for my nighttime nurse that said, "Thanks for loving me tender, you're the best."

Chapter Eighteen
Recovery

I was so happy to be home but so unhappy to be returning to school. I looked like a train wreck and couldn't speak clearly because of my sewn lips. This was going to be a nightmare. What really sucked is that I had to miss all but the first three games of my basketball season.

I went to practice, but Candy Evans wouldn't let me anywhere near the court. If I even looked at a basketball, she would give me the hairy eyeball. My classmates would stare at me, but no one said or did anything hurtful.

One evening I did one of the dumbest things I'd ever done in my life. I hadn't been able to eat any solid food for quite a while and I was hungry. I was looking in the fridge for some chocolate milk when my eyes came to rest on a jar of pickles. Anyone that knows me knows I love dill pickles. I munched on them constantly. The jar sat there begging me to eat some. They were the chip variety, and I thought, "If I take the tube out of the corner of my mouth, I may be able to eat one of these." I pulled the tube out, folded a pickle in half and worked it through the tube hole. I'm not sure how, but it got caught in my throat and I started to choke.

Oh my God, I was going to choke to death on a dill pickle. I couldn't get it back up or force it down. In a panic, I searched for some scissors to cut the stitches out. I was opening drawers and slamming cupboards until the racket brought my mom running into the kitchen.

She took one look at the jar of pickles and knew instantly what had happened. She took her hand and slapped me hard across my back and the offending pickle popped back into my mouth. I worked at it with my tongue until I pushed it back out of the hole, I had put it in with. My mom slapped me across the back again.

"It's okay. It's out," I told her.

"I know," she said, "that one was for being a dumbass."

She was angry and I couldn't blame her. Imagine surviving a major operation only to die trying to eat a pickle. I didn't try to eat anymore but I did drink the juice from a straw.

The swelling in my eyes had started to go down but the damn stitches in my eyelid was driving me nuts. Every time I blinked; I could feel them. It was crazy after all the work I had done that this seemed to bother me the most.

Finally, it was time to go get the stitches out. The ones in my eyelid came out easily and the relief was instant. The ones in my lips had to be plucked out one at a time and it hurt and seemed to take forever. When he finished, Dr. Lehman told me to open my mouth wide.

There are no words in the English language to describe the sensation this caused. I still had no feeling in my upper lip, but it felt very heavy. When I tried to speak, I sounded like the character Mushmouth from the old *Fat Albert* cartoons.

It felt like my lips were getting in the way. Dr. Lehman said it would get better when the swelling subsided and to practice by puckering my lips and singing. Then, he handed me a mirror. Until now, I had been covered in bandages and couldn't see anything but my eyes. Even as swollen as I was, I could see the improvement in my nose. It was much straighter and thinner than it used to be.

I was still a little unsure about what to make of my new top lip. I looked like I had a set of those huge wax lips that you bought at the candystore in my mouth. Dr Lehman said everything would improve in time as the feeling started to return.

When we got home, my mom made a steak for me. Eating turned into a real adventure. I stabbed myself about my mouth with the fork several times. I couldn't feel if it was in my mouth or not. And the corn, forget it. My mom's solution was to set a small tabletop mirror in front of me. It worked like a charm. After a bit of practice, I was getting much more food in my mouth.

When I finished eating, I saw that I had made quite a mess. *I might need a bib, and judging from all the corn on the floor, maybe a highchair.*

Chapter Nineteen
God

I spent a lot of time at home as I continued to heal, I spent most of it watching TV, reading, and listening to music. One evening, I was watching the fire burning in the fireplace and it had a calming, almost hypnotic effect on me, and my thoughts turned to God.

Growing up, I had a complicated relationship with God. I had asked Him repeatedly, "Why me?" Why did I have to have a harelip? Why did I have to suffer all the torment from the other kids? I alternated between hating Him to denying His very existence. My family was not very religious, so it wasn't something we discussed. I stared into the fire seeking answers to my questions.

I had seen some things that made it impossible to deny God's existence. Some breath-taking sunsets, the wonder and beauty of all of nature, people surviving certain death situations. On the other hand, I had seen things and thought there's no way there's a God.

Natural disasters that claimed thousands of lives, innocent children dying, unjustified hatred of people towards their fellow man. What was I to believe? The fire continued to crackle, and the calmness allowed me to ponder these questions without getting upset.

Okay, I thought. *Why was I born with a harelip?*

Could there be a logical reason? Why were some kids born with one arm or blind? "Why were some born beautiful?" Did God simply spin a giant roulette wheel at every birth, and it was all just luck of the draw? If so, I wanted a re-spin. I didn't ask for beautiful, but normal would be nice. The questions kept coming.

Why did God let my brother Mark die? I was seventeen now myself, the same age that he was when he passed. I never got to experience what having a brother was like. Why did my father drown in alcoholism after Mark's death never to recover? Where did my mom find the strength to carry on after his death? Wait. Was I the reason for her strength? She could not allow herself the luxury of going to pieces because she had a four-year-old who needed her.

Finally, why did my sister get to be the beautiful one? I loved Marsha with all my heart, but she was everything I was not. Physically beautiful, extremely smart, funny, and engaging.

Was she just the lucky one? You would never guess we were related. Because she was always so wonderful to me, I can honestly say I was not jealous of her, but I did envy her at times. I'm sure she had her share of hard times and heartache, but I never saw it. To me, she was always my loving, dependable, big sister whom I loved dearly.

I watched as the fire began to die out. This was the first time I had ever been able to think about God without getting angry or blaming him for all my troubles. Then I did something I hadn't done since I was a small child, I prayed. I asked Him to help me find the answers I was seeking and to help me find some peace.

I don't tell this story to sound preachy or suggest I had some life-changing epiphany, I believe that everyone's relationship with God is personal. I tell it because I did find some peace that night and my relationship with God became markedly improved after that. Was God talking to me that night? Maybe so. He was a hell of a listener.

Chapter Twenty
The Ice Cream Social

I stayed home, except for school, all the time. Venturing out in public with my bandages and black eyes wasn't something I was comfortable with. Friends would stop to visit, but for the most part I sat in the house bored to death.

Keith stopped by one evening and said, "Let's go out for some ice cream."

I looked at him like he had taken leave of his senses. I looked a little better by then but was still not ready to put myself on public display.

"No way," I told him.

He begged me to go the Friendly's Ice Cream with him which was just around the corner from the house.

"Keith, this is going to be a disaster," I pleaded.

He tried to cheer me up by saying I just looked like I was in a car crash.

"Well, that makes me feel better," I replied sarcastically.

He promised me he would help me eat without making too big a mess, and we would leave at the first sign of trouble. So, off we went.

I couldn't shake the feeling of impending doom as we walked in the door. The hostess stared at me in sheer horror as she led us to our table. Everyone was looking at us, but Keith pretended not to notice. The waitress came over to take our order and when she asked Keith what he wanted, he completely ignored her.

She turned to me very confused.

"He's hard of hearing," I said, unable to come up with any other reason.

"WHAT CAN I GET FOR YOU SIR," she practically screamed at him.

"Banana split please," he yelled back. When I started giggling at him, he said, "Good to hear you laugh again."

We ate our sundaes in relative peace until a woman and her two teenage daughters sat down in the booth behind us. A dark look crossed Keith's face and when I turned to see what he was looking at, the girls were putting their napkins over their faces like my bandages.

"Ignore them," I whispered to myself.

Then the mother said loudly, "How can he eat with that thing sitting with him?"

Now I was angry. Keith asked for the check making good on his promise to leave at the first sign of trouble. I lit a cigarette in an effort to calm down and keep my mouth shut.

We got up to leave just as the waitress was setting their sundaes on the table. It was an opportunity I just couldn't pass up. I stopped right there and put my cigarette out right in the middle of the mother's ice cream. She couldn't have been more shocked if I'd had slapped her, a thought that did cross my mind.

Behind me, Keith exploded in laughter. He dipped his finger into the whipped cream of one of the girls' sundaes and stuck it in his mouth. With that, we made our exit.

In the car, we laughed hysterically at our antics. It wasn't my proudest moment, but damn was it funny.

"Thanks for having my back," I said.

He stopped laughing and said, "I'll always have your back."

Chapter Twenty-One
Adults can be Bullies Too

I was getting better at ignoring people who were bothering me. The stares and the occasional hurtful remarks were getting easier to deal with. I learned however, that when you hurt my mother, I could become a monster.

I was out Christmas shopping one day when I decided to stop by the bowling alley where my mom was bowling in her league. We sat at the table, and I was showing her some of the gifts I had bought.

This guy named Jim walked by and pointed at me and said, "My God Janice, what happened to her?"

My mom and I both stared at him dumbfounded. "Nothing happened to her," my mom replied icily.

"Well, she looks like someone hit her in the face with a shovel."

My mom said sternly, "That's enough Jim, be on your way."

All the old anger and fight that I was trying so hard to leave behind came rushing back to the surface.

I jumped to my feet and said, "Yeah Jim, be on your way."

Tears began to gather at the corner of my eyes. My mom stood up and got between us.

Then she completely shocked me when she said to me, "Just ignore him, he's a fucking drunk."

My mother NEVER said the f word. She hated it and I avoided saying it in front of her. I was still glaring at Jim trying to decide what to do. My mom put her hands on both sides of my face and forced me to look at her instead.

Tears were falling down her cheeks, and she looked deep into my eyes and whispered in a quivering voice, "Please."

As much as I wanted to grab a bowling ball and cram it down Jim's throat, I didn't want to embarrass my mom in front of her friends. I looked back at Jim and said again, "Be on your way Jim, before I drop you where you stand."

He staggard off mumbling to himself. I kissed my mom and said, "I better go." I really didn't want her to see how hurt I was.

My mom sat at the table crying when her good friend Millie came over to ask her what was wrong. My mom told her, and I guess Millie took matters into her own hands. She cornered this idiot and chewed him out. Some of mom's other friends, after learning what happened, joined in. Mom told me it was so bad, that Jim left the bowling alley without finishing his third game.

Mom called me when she got home and told me she was proud of me for not stomping Jim's guts out because she didn't want me to get arrested. I teased her about her "potty" mouth and called her my gansta momma. I told her I was okay, and she didn't need to worry about me.

The following week at bowling Jim apologized to my mom. She told me he said he didn't know what came over him.

"Did you accept it," I asked her.

"No," she said laughing. "I told him to blow it out his fucking ass."

Way to go mom.

Chapter Twenty-Two
Not Again

I awoke one morning to a searing pain on the left side of my nose. I couldn't draw any air through it either. My first thought was, I must have a hell of a sinus infection. I did the whole Vicks Vapor Rub routine and took a bunch of decongestants, but nothing seemed to help.

By nightfall the pain was getting worse. I tried warm compresses, steam, whatever else I could think of. I didn't get a wink of sleep that night and by morning, I was in agony. I was lucky enough to get an emergency appointment with my family doctor.

After examining me she said, "I believe the left side of your sinus cavity has collapsed."

Are you freaking kidding me? She gave me something for the pain and had her office make an appointment with a local plastic surgeon for the next day.

I won't mention his name because somehow, he managed to turn this into a bigger mess. He took some x-rays and found that my sinus had indeed collapsed. I was just sick about it. Surgery was scheduled for two days later. I hated having to tell my mom that I needed another operation.

"It might not be so bad this time," I told her. It was same-day surgery, and I would be home that night. The plan was to take some cartilage from behind my ear and use it to rebuild my sinus cavity. Piece of cake.

I arrived at the hospital on surgery day worried but not scared to death like I was the first time. There was no time for Act Two of my Elvis impersonation show this time. Back into the OR I went for round two. When I awoke, my nose was packed again but I wasn't hooked up to a bunch of tubes like a science experiment. After an hour, I was released to go home with instructions not to strain or lift anything heavy.

I had an appointment in one week to return to have the packing removed. I made sure to take it easy to allow my nose to heal properly. When he did remove the packing, the pain was gone, and I could breathe again. All was right with the world again. At least for a month or two when it happened again.

I noticed over time that I was having trouble breathing again. Another doctor visit showed that my sinus hadn't collapsed but the ear cartilage wasn't strong enough to hold it open. He wanted to go in again and try to repair it but this time I told him I wanted a second opinion. This seemed to really piss him off, so I set out to find a new surgeon.

Chapter Twenty-Three
The Soap Oprea Lady

Setting out to find a new surgeon proved to be a bit difficult. Most doctors did not want to fix something that another one had screwed up.

Lynda Hirsch was a television personality on a local station out of Cleveland. She hosted a segment giving updates on all the soap operas. My mom always tuned in to find out who the father of Jane's baby was, or if the affair between Bill and Mary would be discovered.

One day, she talked about some plastic surgery she had done. She looked great and my mom got an idea. She called the station and left a message for Lynda explaining the situation and asking her for the name of the doctor who had done her work.

To her everlasting credit, Lynda called my mom back and spoke with her. She gave mom the name of her surgeon, Dr. Bahman Guyuron out of Cleveland. Next thing I knew, I was off to see the man.

When we arrived at his office, we both stood in the doorway and looked around. The decorations, furniture, and marble tile were out of this world. The place even smelled expensive. I felt underdressed. I checked in and we waited for my name to be called.

Soon, a very beautiful assistant named Thersa escorted us to an exam room. She looked like she had been carved out of porcelain. Every feature, including her skin, was flawless. The room was so plush, none of those industrial exam tables here, it looked more like a couch. I was taken for x-rays then sent back to the room to await the doctor.

Dr Guyuron came in. He was a pleasant man but when he started to talk about everything he wanted to do.

I thought, *Wow, I'm more messed up than I thought I was.*

The surgery was going to be a lot more extensive than I thought. The ear cartilage was not strong enough to hold so he was going to take a piece of my rib and use that. He wanted to make some improvements to my nose and cheekbones to contour my face a bit better.

I looked over at my mom and said, "You ready to do this again?"

She smiled and said, "I am if you are."

With that, I was scheduled for yet another surgery.

By now, I was becoming an old pro at this. Back to the hospital I went to literally have my face rearranged again. My nose was broken yet again, and my cheekbones were broken and realigned and my eyes turned black again. The big difference this time was the ride home.

During the surgery I had swallowed a lot of blood and had the dry heaves all the way home. I was gagging and the pressure made my nose bleed and my eyes water. My mom started crying and my poor friend, who was driving was a nervous wreck.

We had to pull over at an intersection so I could throw up. I was bent over puking with my door hanging open and my head down. A man who worked at a nearby car dealership came running over to see what was wrong. When I looked up at him, he recoiled in complete horror. I had blood all over my bandaged face, tears running from my black eyes, and I scared the poor guy half to death. My mom got out and told him I was alright, but it shook him up pretty badly.

Everything worked out and my breathing issues were gone. My face, with its rebuilt nose and cheekbones, looked more symmetrical. When the swelling went away, and I looked in the mirror I decided I was satisfied with the way I looked. I would never be mistaken for a model, but I could go out in public without drawing stares or unwelcomed comments. I was done with surgery.

Famous last words.

Chapter Twenty-Four
Keith Revisited

Keith and I hung out for all my high school years. He was the kindest, funniest, most unusual person I had ever met. I have never known anyone like him. He honestly didn't give a damn what anyone thought of him. He spoke his mind, laughed at anything he found funny, and was my biggest cheerleader.

He was determined to bring me out of my shell. He put me in situations that forced me to interact with people. One of his favorite tricks was to refuse to introduce me when we met someone, forcing me to introduce myself.

Whenever I put my hands in front of my face when I spoke, he would reach and pull them down. When I spoke to him without making eye contact, he would gently put his hand under my chin and turn me to face him. I'll be honest, there were times when I felt like a stray pet he had adopted, but I knew his heart was in the right place.

My dad didn't like him, but my dad seemed to hate any boy I talked to. My mom didn't quite know what to make of him.

He would call my house and say things like, "Hi, Mrs. Laschinske, will you tell Amy she left her panties in my car again."

My sister saw all the good he was doing me, so she adored him. He did, inadvertently, almost get me killed once.

He was a year older than me, so I went through my senior year without him. We didn't have cellphones back then so if he wanted me to call him, he would call the school and ask them to have me call Dr. Westhill to discuss my test results.

I would receive a note from the office with a number, (Keith's) to return the call. One day, I came home from school to find my mom in tears and my sitter glaring at me.

My mom yelled, "Do you have something you want to tell me young lady?"

My mind raced to find something I might have done to anger her this way. "Not that I can think of," I replied.

Marsha grabbed me by the arm and said, "Are you pregnant?"

My jaw hit the floor. "What makes you think I'm pregnant?"

My mom produced the note from the fictious Dr. Westhill telling me she found this in my pocket while she was doing laundry. Had they not been so mad, I would have laughed.

"No, I am not pregnant."

My mom demanded to know why then, this doctor was calling me and what tests he was talking about.

I said, "Mom, it's not a doctor, it's Keith."

I thought her head might explode right then. She chewed my ass out but good. She ended by saying I should thank God I wasn't a few years younger, or she'd take a belt to me.

Keith went off to college and as expected, we began to drift apart. One night he called me and said he had something to talk to me about. He came over to my house and when I saw the look on his face, I knew it was serious.

He took my hands in his and said, "Amy, I'm gay."

I burst out laughing but when his eyes filled with tears, I stopped. He had met someone at college and was happy. He said what we had was real and that he really did love me, but he had to be true to himself.

"Keith, we talked about getting married and having kids for Christ sakes."

He swore that he honestly believed that that was the way things were going to be. I was torn between wanting to hug him or punching him in the face. He told me he would give me time to process all this, but he really hoped we could remain friends. With a quick peck on my cheek, he was gone.

We talked on and off for a few years. I couldn't deny the importance he had played in my life. He seemed happy and I was happy for him. The calls became less frequent over time, each of us busy with our own lives.

One day, after not hearing from him for a while. He called my house out of the blue. He told me he really needed to see me.

"What's up?" I asked.

He told me he was dying of aids and that it was important that he see me. I was in shock. But agreed to meet him at his parents' house the next day.

Nothing could have prepared me for the scene that awaited me when I walked into his room. I felt my knees buckle a little. He was lying in a hospital bed with an oxygen mask on. He was half the size he used to be, and his skin was an ashy, gray color.

Putting on the bravest face I could muster. I walked over to him. He smiled weakly when he saw me and patted the side of his bed. He removed the mask from his face and started to speak, asking me not to interrupt him so he could get it all out.

"When you're dying," he began, "Your life plays over and over like a movie. I want you to know you were the star of my show. I love you so much and I need you to make a promise to me right now."

I took his hand and nodded.

"Don't let your harelip define you. Open up and show people the Amy I know. Don't put that wall back up."

I promised him I would do as he asked. Then it was my turn to speak. I told him I could never repay him for everything he did for me, all the gifts he gave me, the laughter, the self-confidence. I could never had made it this far without him. Consider me his legacy. He was starting to get tired, and I really needed to get out of there before I completely went to pieces.

"I love you, Keith, and I'll never forget you." I kissed him on the forehead and walked out of the room.

Three days later, he was gone.

I think of him often. It wasn't the fairy tale ending I had hoped for, but that's life. Every now and then, especially when I meet new people, I will absentmindedly put my hands in front of my face, and I swear I can feel him pulling them down. It was my privilege and honor to have known this wonderful man. RIP

Chapter Twenty-Five
Speaking of Gay

This chapter may offend some of you so let me apologize in advance. All the events I've described thus far have been true and I see no sense in not telling the truth now. I discovered very late in life, and much to my surprise, that I too am gay. (Keith would have found this hysterical). After I lost Keith, I didn't think I would ever find love again. I resigned myself to the fact that I would be alone for the rest of my life and worked hard to be okay with that.

Even though my social skills had improved, I was not charming or outgoing. I still wasn't comfortable talking to anyone I didn't know. The word most often used to describe me then was quiet. It took me a long time to learn to trust people and I suppose that made me seem distant and cold. Despite my promise to Keith, I had indeed rebuilt the wall around my heart.

I met Pam at a bowling alley on a Friday night. I was walking past the table where she sat, and our eyes met, and she smiled at me. The first thing I noticed was that she had a gap between her front teeth that I found adorable. I continued walking but something made me stop and turn around. I had no idea what I was going to do but when I got to her, I asked her if I could buy her a beer. I felt like someone else was controlling me.

"Sure," she replied and flashed a smile again.

I grabbed us two beers and sat down at her table. We talked for the rest of the evening. It was completely out of character for me. As I was leaving, I said I hoped to see her again, she said she was there every Friday.

I won't go into too much detail about how a great friendship turned into a love affair, but I will tell you that we have been together nearly twenty-eight years now. I struggled with it at first. I didn't want to be gay. I had gay friends, and their lifestyle made no difference to me, but it wasn't for me. Finally, I realized that I loved Pam, and it changed my life.

The point of the story is that even though I always felt ugly, self-conscious, and inferior to everyone, I found love. Pam erased all of that. She claims to have never noticed the harelip; said she noticed my eyes first. She got me to talk about things that I would never discuss with anyone else. She helped me heal.

I'm not advocating for or condemning my lifestyle; the point is it works for me. No matter what your self-image is, there is a love out there for you and it will change your entire perspective of life. Never give up on your happiness.

Chapter Twenty-Six
The Last Surgery

Pam and I were sitting at home one afternoon when I got a phone call from Dr. Guyuron's office. They told me about a technique the doctor was performing called dermabrasion. It basically meant that he would grind a layer of skin off your face to make it smoother and lighten the scars.

It was safer than a chemical peel which could cause issues with pigmentation. They asked if this would be something I would be interested in. I told them I would call them back. I knew this would be a tricky issue to bring up to Pam.

She was constantly reassuring me that I looked fine, but they had me at, lightening my scars. Even though I knew I looked better than before, every time I looked in a mirror all I could see were the scars. I wanted to jump at the chance to minimize them. Pam, however had a different point of view when I brought this all up.

"What the hell is wrong with you?" she asked. "Haven't you been through enough?" She had her arms folded across her chest and was having none of it.

"What's wrong with wanting to look better?" I asked. Then I tried teasing her, "Wouldn't you want a cute girlfriend?"

"I already have one," she replied.

"Yeah, what's her name?" I quickly realized that this

approach was going nowhere. We discussed the whole thing at length, and I finally convinced her to at least come and talk to the doctor with me.

Unbelievably, when we walked into the waiting room, Lynda Hirsch, the soap opera lady, was in there. I was thrilled with the opportunity to thank her in person for leading us to Dr. Guyuron. She was such a class act that I even started watching her TV segments, even though I didn't give a damn about soap operas.

We went into an exam room and Dr. Guyuron explained the procedure to us. I looked over at Pam who shrugged her shoulders and told me to go ahead if I wanted to.

Back to the O.R. I went. When I woke up, I felt like someone had thrown gasoline in my face and set fire to it. The burning was incredible. Imagine being dragged, face down, across concrete. My face was covered in what looked like melted candle wax. Of all the surgeries I had gone through, this one was the most painful.

Because the doctor wanted to see me the next day, Pam and I opted to stay in a hotel near his office. We got our room key and when we went inside, we both looked around in disgust. I've been in cleaner port-a-potties.

We literally stuck to the floor. We didn't dare take our shoes off. We looked at the stained bedspread and Pam said, "No way." She went out to the car and got the emergency blanket out and laid it across the bed.

In the meantime, I was bitching and moaning about all of it just to be helpful. We lay on the blanket and watched TV until we both fell asleep. We went to my post op checkout and headed home.

I had to wear this wax mask thing for a week. It was the longest week of my life. I was miserable. My skin underneath the mask itched like crazy. It nearly drove me insane but all I could do was bitch about it, which drove Pam insane.

Finally, I went to get the mask off, and my face was the color of bright red dye. It honestly looked like I had been burnt in a fire. They gave me all kind of creams to rub on my face that helped with the itch and eventually, my face turned into a more normal color.

Pam and I had a long talk after that. She begged me not to put myself through this anymore. I looked fine and she didn't see where any of this was worth it. I confessed that I was disappointed in the results. The scars didn't look all that different to me. She was right.

This was as good as it was going to get and in truth, I was okay with that. I was going to give up on my dream of becoming a super model and return to the life of the steelworker that I was.

Chapter Twenty-Seven
Jy Is Genoeg

Jy Is Genoeg is Afrikaans meaning You Are Enough in English. I'd like to tell you how this simple phrase began the process of me turning my life around.

I was listening to music on YouTube one day when I was led to a video by an extremely talented, South African, singer named Liezel Pieters. The song, which I believe she wrote, was "*Jy Is Genoeg*."

I didn't understand the words, but the video sent a clear message. It depicted a woman who was physically and verbally abused by her husband to the point where she considered taking her own life. The message said that no one should ever be made feel inferior, unworthy, or undeserving of love and respect. When I was growing up, my mom always told me I was good enough, but I always thought she had to say that because she was my mom. Hearing this song made me think of her and struck a chord in my soul.

On her Facebook page, Miss Pieters encouraged her fans to write this message on the palm of their hands in support of any woman who needed to hear it. I, feeling the message was far too important, decided to have it tattooed on my left forearm, so off to the tattoo parlor I went.

I wrestled with the decision of whether to have it done in English or Afrikaans. I settled on Afrikaans for one reason, anyone who saw it would be forced to ask me what it meant. It could be a chance to help spread the message or maybe open a conversation with a stranger who just needed someone to talk to. The response has been so satisfying.

I can't count the number of people who've asked me about it. Speaking to one young lady who had been badly burnt on her face left us both in tears but was so rewarding. It also forced me to become far more social than I was comfortable with but was well worth it. Whenever I find myself in a place of doubt, or too scared to speak up, I glance at my arm and dive right in.

So, I just wanted to give Liezel Pieters a shout out for sending a message that meant so much to me and helped me find my voice. I imagine the whole point of writing a song is to touch the folks you wrote it for, and you have done that. I really like the person I'm becoming because of it.

Chapter Twenty-Eight
The Lobster Family

I read an article somewhere about how freak shows were starting to make a comeback. Suddenly, a childhood memory filled my brain against my will. It reminded me of an event that left me traumatized when I was around eight years old.

I was at a local fair with my friends when we decided to go see the freak show. The colorful banners showed a picture of lobsters with human faces on them. The barker told us that we should come see the incredible lobster family, we wouldn't believe our eyes. We coughed up our fifty cents each and went into the tent.

It was dark inside and a little spooky. When the curtain was drawn, there in the spotlight, were three severely deformed human beings. It was a father and his two children. They had no arms or legs but a small fin like appendage instead. They were lying on a bed of straw and flopping around for the audience. People, including my friends, were laughing and pointing at them. One of the kids came flopping over to me and our eyes met.

I will never forget the profound sadness on his face. Lobster boy, meet Rabbit girl. (For those who don't know, the term harelip is used to describe someone with a cleft lip and palate because of the resemblance to the lip of a rabbit.) I turned and ran out of the tent and went and threw up in the nearest trash can.

My young brain could not process what I had just seen. I was angry, sad, and confused all at the same time. When my friends found me, I told them I was sick from eating too much junk. I went through the motions the rest of the evening, riding rides, playing games, but the image of Lobster Boy and I staring at each other haunted me.

When my parents came to pick me up, they knew something was wrong. I was unusually quiet for a kid who had just come from a fun night out. My dad asked me if I had fun and I said, "Yeah, except for the Lobster Family."

"Who the hell is the Lobster family?" he asked.

I told him all about the scene I had witnessed. Because I was only eight, he had a hard time trying to explain it to me. He told me people were curious about stuff like this.

"Why would they sit in a tent and let people come in to make fun of them?" I asked.

He said that the daddy had to make some money for his family. I just couldn't comprehend it.

I thought about Lobster Boy at the most unexpected times for months. When I was out playing baseball or whatever I would think about how he couldn't do any of this. I wondered if he went to school, or could he talk. It was also the first time in my life when I realized that having a harelip was not the worst thing in the world.

I eventually forgot about the Lobster family until that day I read the article. I hope it's not true.

Chapter Twenty-Nine
South Africa

I took a vacation to Cape Town, South Africa last February and it was life-changing for me. I had retired from my job in the steel mill where I worked for over thirty years, and I was restless and felt lost. I didn't know what I was going to do with the rest of my life.

My friend Jan, who I met in high school when she was an exchange student, invited me to visit her in Cape Town, South Africa. Pam was unable to travel due to health problems, so my dear friend Angie came along.

I had visited Jan and her husband Michel, whom I call Siggy, twice before. Once in Zimbabwe and once in Johannesburg, but that was almost thirty years before. Plans were made and Angie and I hopped a flight for Cape Town.

I was so happy to see Jan and Siggy and their kids again. Nicole, their oldest, was my god daughter and I hadn't seen their other two kids. Jenna and Marc, since they were little kids. We drove to their house in George, and I got to see Jan's mother Fay, whom I adore, again as well.

Jan is one of the most extraordinary people I have ever met. Nicole was born with Downs Syndrome and unable to find suitable schooling for her, Jan and her family built one. The Up with Downs school for special need learners started out with four students in Jan's garage and has grown into a sprawling campus that spans a few city blocks.

When we visited there, I was in awe. How amazing what a woman with a dream can accomplish. The whole family is involved in the day-to-day operation of the school, and I couldn't have been more impressed.

South Africa is a beautiful country. The mountains and ocean and the animals were just breath-taking. But the thing that impressed me the most was the people. Everyone I met was so warm and friendly. I commented to Jan that they were so much more friendly than in the States. While I enjoyed all of this, the biggest impact was the conversations I had with Jan and her mom Fay.

I told them I was feeling off. I felt like I was looking for something, but I didn't know what it was. I also told them that even though I am sixty-one years old, I still had trouble talking to strangers. We decided that I needed to practice my social skills while I was there. We conducted a kind of social experiment. I went out on the balcony of our hotel alone to smoke.

All the tables were full, so I stood along the railing and lit a cigarette. I heard a man's voice behind me say, "Excuse me miss, please join me at my table." I turned to find him pointing at an empty chair.

I sat down and I thought, *Talk to this man. Don't be an idiot.*

His name was Fabio, and we talked for nearly an hour. Jan got worried and came looking for me.

I introduced her to my new friend and when we left Jan said, "See what happens when you open your mouth."

I talked to a lot of people and was delighted by the results. When I was talking to Fay, I told her I was thinking about writing a book.

She said, "You must do it."

We set a date for me to visit them again in 2026. I said I would return in better health, as a non-smoker, and an author. I intend to keep that date.

Angie and I had so much fun on our vacation. We visited a safari, did a few wine tastings, and visited many small towns. It was Angie's first visit to Africa, and it was fun watching her experience it for the first time. She also took some amazing pictures.

I returned home with a new sense of purpose. I made myself be kinder and more open to everyone. I found a renewed joy in writing and took up the cause to end bullying. Friends I had known for years commented on how I seemed so different since my trip. So, a great big thank you to all the Seegmullers, Angie, and Fay for pointing me in the right direction. Even I don't recognize this new and improved version of myself. Nicole, you own my heart.

Chapter Thirty
Bullying

I didn't write this book to become a famous author. I wrote it for anyone, especially a young person who is dealing with a troubling issue. I hope you can find some solutions or inspirations in my words. I'm not an expert, I don't have a degree in psychology, I'm just a girl who has been in your shoes and knows your pain.

The latest statistic I have seen, says that 4,500 kids under the age of sixteen, commit suicide due to bullying each year. I came so close to being one of those kids. I finally reached a point where my silence on the subject was giving my consent to this. I had to find a way to join the fight to end it. I realized that the best contribution was for me to tell my story in the hopes that it reaches the people who need to hear it.

I don't care how pretty you are, how wealthy, what your social status is, bullying anyone you think is beneath you is wrong. The girl born with no legs, is just as important as the prom queen.

The boy who wears the same clothes with holes in them, is just as important as the football captain. It just boils down to basic decency. Until you can offer me real proof that bullying someone somehow improves your life, I won't accept it.

I don't care how high up the ladder you climb; you

couldn't get there without the first rung. I don't care if you're the CEO of the company or the janitor, you both play a role in the success of the company.

I'm not innocent. I have looked at a homeless person on the street in disgust. I have bullied other people for various reasons. I'm not trying to lecture you. All I'm suggesting is that we learn to treat others with respect and less judgement. I have finally learned that to be kind to others is so much more rewarding.

When I started coaching basketball to junior high school girls years ago, I always rooted for the underdogs. I of course, cheered the efforts of my star players, I liked to win. But the memories I cherish the most had nothing to do with winning or losing. The joy and excitement of the least athletic girl on the team scoring her first basket then running over to me and hugging me. It doesn't get any better than that. Those are the kids I remember best.

I cursed the fact that I was born with a cleft lip. I spent much of my life being defensive and angry about it. Now I view it as more of an opportunity. I can add something useful to the fight against childhood suicide and bullying. It's a subject that I can offer some insight into. My only regret is that it took me so long to see it.

My heart aches for all the children we have lost to suicide. Lives that will never be realized. Did we lose the one who would finally find a cure for cancer? The one who could figure out how to end world hunger. We will never know what their contributions to society could have been. When a young child feels that taking their own life is the only way out, something is horribly wrong. When I learned of the story of a twelve-year-old girl who killed herself after being bullied, I wrote a few poems for her and all the other children we have lost. They can be found in the next chapter. I hope they convey the urgency we need to end this fight.

Chapter Thirty-One
Poems

These poems are dedicated to all the children we have lost to suicide due to bullying.

Say Their Name

Saying their name is fine
But the memories fade over time
We forget all their pain and their tears
Soon the days and the months become years
How did we miss their cries
When did compassion die
We must do better. We all must try
Raise your voice, sound the battle cry
Those beautiful souls needlessly lost
Silence comes at too steep a cost
Let's all rise, rise up my friends
Bring all their suffering to an end.

Echoes in the Wind

When they fight alone, they cannot win
We'll hear the echoes in the wind
Help me, hear me, rescue me
Blowing softly in the breeze
The pain, the fear, the agony

Was always there, we didn't see
Haunted voices we didn't hear
Will fill the raindrops with their tears
Lives were wasted, not to grow
Colder than the winter snow
So be a beacon, be their sun
Until we have this battle won
Or be their moon, cast a light
Help them live, help them fight.

It's Too Late Then

When I am hanging from a rope
Out of faith, out of hope
Never knowing what might have been
Don't offer help, it's too late then
When the gun is in my hand
To end the pain, I can't withstand
I've gone as far as I can bend
Don't cry for me, it's too late then
When I am lying in my grave
There's nothing left for you to save
Cards and flowers you will send
Don't pray for me, it's too late then
We must do something, you will cry
Another child must not die
We have to make this madness end
Don't fight for me, it's too late then

Chapter Thirty-Two
Pointers

It's important for you to know that I did not write this book to become a famous author. I tell my story for anyone who experienced bullying who may find some hope or inspiration in my words. I want to offer a few tips to help you get by. I'm not an expert and these tips should not be construed as expert advice. Think of them as pointers from a woman who has been there. I have stood in your shoes and felt your pain. Over the years, here are some things I have learned.

One, learn to respect and love yourself. Whatever problems you have, be they physical or emotional, they do not make you ugly, they only make you different. I remember standing beside my dad when I was a kid, admiring a beautiful Thunderbird automobile. When my dad started looking at the engine, I asked him why.

He said, "A beautiful car is only as good as the engine under the hood."

Remember that. Some of the "prettiest" people you meet will be the ugliest human beings.

Think of some of the celebrities we admire, if you take away the make-up, the hairstylist, and the fancy clothes, you will find that they look like ordinary people. I'm not saying it's wrong to want to look your best, I'm suggesting that beauty is often an illusion.

Despite any flaw you may have, you can still be beautiful.

Two, you are beneath no one. Never let anyone make you feel unworthy or undeserving of love and respect. Always remember Jy Is Genoeg (You Are Enough.) You have as much right to be happy as anyone else. Demand that you be treated with basic respect. Regardless of wealth, beauty, social status, we are all simply human beings. No one is better than you.

Three, find someone you trust that you can share your thoughts and feelings with. We all need someone we can talk to about anything. Find someone who makes you feel safe. If you can't, it's perfectly acceptable to seek professional help. There is nothing wrong with seeing a therapist.

Four, observe the people around you. Actions truly do speak louder than words. I love music and when I find a singer I like, I can honestly say I couldn't care less what they look like. I go to their Facebook page and try to figure out what kind of person they are, what do their fans admire about them, etc. For me, it's about the talent not the appearance. Find people who display traits you admire, honesty, integrity, and compassion, to name a few. These are the people you want to befriend.

Five, open up. This was the hardest thing for me to learn to do. I spent years with a protective wall around me. I believed it to be the best way to keep myself from being hurt. The result was that I didn't let people get to know the real me. My need to protect myself made me seem cold and unapproachable. When I finally did learn to let people in, I formed friendships that have lasted a lifetime. I found humor worked for me. People automatically like you more if you're funny. There are times as you become more open when you are going to be fooled, betrayed, and even have your heartbroken, it happens sometimes. But it's worth it to take the chance.

Six, find something you are passionate about that brings you joy. For me it was sports but for you maybe its singing or dancing. Maybe reading or knitting, it doesn't matter. Doing something you enjoy is a great way to relieve stress and help you gain some self-confidence.

This is not a complete list; these are just a few things I've learned over the years that helped me cope. I carried around so much anger for years. It was very self-destructive; I only began to heal when I let it go. The one thing I can promise you is that your life will not always be the shitshow of your youth. I tell you this from experience. I can honestly say that aside from the fact that I still can't play the damn slide trombone, my cleft lip and palate has zero influence on my life today. Stay strong!

Chapter Thirty-Three
Wrapping it Up

There you have it folks, the good, the bad, and the ugly stories that made up my life to this point. I did not write my stories to illicit any pity from you. I wrote it because I realized that by remaining silent, I was giving my consent to bullying and it's a subject I know a lot about.

If whoever reads this book finds inspiration and hope in my words, I will be completely satisfied. I know that there are a lot of good, decent, people out there, I just wish it hadn't taken me so long to see them. I was blinded by my own anger and mistrust due to being treated so poorly by a select few, I fought my way through, and I know you can too. As you grow older, you will find that it's worth the journey.

I don't mean to suggest that I am perfect, far from it. I am still learning new life lessons every day. I am still learning how to be a better person and it's not always easy. I still have moments when I am judgmental, unreasonable, and unwilling to listen to people whom I do not agree with.

The difference is that I am much more aware of it now and I am working to do better. My temper has always been an issue I fought with. Like a wild animal who felt trapped and threatened.

I lashed out. I understood where the anger came from,

but it was sometimes uncalled for and inexcusable. I have learned to think before I speak now or to simply walk away from a situation when I feel my ire rise. I now realize how my words, spoken in anger, can hurt someone. If I ever hurt your feelings, I am truly sorry.

Your future is what you make it. In spite of the torment I went through, I have led a pretty good life that I am grateful for. I have loved and been loved by some wonderful people, I have seen some amazing places, I have experienced some things that made me weep with joy. None of this would have happened if I had been successful in my suicide attempt at the age of twelve. Keep fighting, you have a lot to live for.

I found my way through by finding humor, empathy, and kindness towards my fellow man. If I can help, I will. If you're struggling with something and ask for advice or a sympathetic ear, I'm your girl. If you need cheering up, I'm your clown. It cost nothing and doesn't have to be a monumental gesture. Sometimes a smile is all that's needed. I have learned that the better version of myself that I put out there, the better people I attract.

I don't care what your issue is, a physical deformity, mental issues, addiction, whatever, everybody has one, and you can overcome it. It will take patience, courage, and heart. There will be times when you will want to give up, times when you will cry, times when you think the pain will never end. I promise you that this is very normal. Fight your way through, and if you need help, ask for it. Don't waste years, as I did, letting all the negative issues rule your life. Every climb up the ladder begins with the first rung. Start today. I know you can do it.

About the Author

Amy Laschinske is a retired steelworker who currently resides in Massillon, Ohio with her long-time partner Pam and their dog, Zippy. She has no other qualifications for writing this book other than she has lived through it.

She welcomes all questions or feedback to CoachAmy05@ aol.com or to her Facebook page.

Printed in the USA
CPSIA information can be obtained
at www.ICGtesting.com
LVHW050731051224
798286LV00002B/164